SOCCER RUFUS
and the Big Debut

National Library of Australia
Cataloguing-in-Publication entry

Creator: Beck, Adrian, author, illustrator.
Title: Soccerufus and the big debut / Adrian Beck, author and illustrator;
        Archie Thompson, contributor; Geoff Slattery, editor.
ISBN: 9780987342812 (paperback)
Target Audience: For primary school age.
Subjects: Thompson, Archie.
            Soccer players--Juvenile fiction.
            School sports--Juvenile fiction.
            Soccer teams--Juvenile fiction.
            Soccer stories.
Other Creators/Contributors: Thompson, Archie.
                            Slattery, Geoff, editor.
Dewey Number: A823.4

Group Publisher: Geoff Slattery
Project Manager: Marlo Mercuri
Editor: Geoff Slattery
Designer: Chris Downey
Cover Design: Adrian Beck
Cover photograph of Archie Thompson: Chris Downey
Illustration on page 145 by Olivia Beck, the author's 4YO daughter

Printed and bound in Australia by McPherson's Printing Group

The Slattery Media Group Pty Ltd
1 Albert Street, Richmond, Victoria, Australia 3121
www.slatterymedia.com

SOCCERUFUS
and the Big Debut

Adrian Beck with Archie Thompson

FROM THE AUTHORS...

Hi kids, Archie here!

In my 54 games for the Socceroos and 254 for Melbourne Victory I've had some pretty incredible moments, but bringing you this brand new book, *Soccerufus*, is definitely another career highlight for me. I'm passionate about the growth of football in Australia and I hope this story might play a small part in inspiring the next generation of players—that's you!— to get out on the pitch and give it your best shot.

There's so much to love about football. It helps you make friends, brings communities together, gets you active, teaches you how to work as a team and can lead to lifelong memories. But most of all it's great fun to play.

Happy reading and happy playing!

Archie Thompson

Hello soccer fans, Adrian here!

I never quite had the same unbelievable soccer career as Archie, but I did slog it out for the Eastern Shore Saints Junior Soccer Club in Tasmania all through primary school. I was far from the best player on the team but I loved every minute of it.

The character in this story is named Rufus. He's new to the game of soccer and hasn't developed his skills just yet. What I like most about him, is that he tries hard and stays positive no matter what happens. On any team, that approach can be just as important as being the most skilful.

Hope you enjoy the story!

Adrian Beck

To Isabella and Axel,

For keeping me young and making me proud.

AT

For Jane,

How lucky I am to have you on my side.

AB

CONTENTS

1

THE CLINIC

The name's Rufus. SOCCERufus.

Not so long ago, my whole life changed due to one amazing moment. It was Friday 26th February, 2016, the day Archie Thompson and the Socceroos visited our school. Nothing would be the same again.

It all started at assembly, when Principal Humpton explained, in between the rumblings coming from his big round belly, what a huge deal the clinic would be. We called him Humpty behind his back. But to me he was more of a jolly old Santa Claus, without the fluffy beard. When he laughed his tummy wobbled big time.

Principal Humpty reminded everyone that until then the most exciting sporting event held at Bayview had been when the school—students and staff—attempted to set a hoola-hoop world record.

I happened to catch the hoola-hoop record attempt on TV when I was still living out in the country. The whole thing was called off when Principal Humpty got his hoop STUCK. Oooops.

But to have Archie Thompson and the Socceroos showing their skills was something else. Even though I wasn't really into soccer, and definitely wasn't on the school team, I knew it would be MASSIVE to have the stars of the sport showing us how to play, but I couldn't have guessed just how MASSIVE it would be for me.

My classmate Dash, was totally pumped. She was
a star of the school team and she knew all about the
Socceroos and Archie. "Archie's a *proper* world record
holder," she whispered. She may have been super shy and
occasionally a bit of a stutterer, but she was the smartest
kid in our class. "Archie is the highest-scoring Socceroo
ever. He booted 13 goals in one match against American
Samoa. Most players don't manage that in a lifetime!"

Some kids have a love for sport from an early age.
And that's cool, but that just wasn't me. Not because
I've ever had anything against sport, but until recently
I'd been a country kid who used to take an hour's bus
ride to and from school. When that's your routine it
doesn't leave much time for after school activities.
Besides, any spare moments I had were spent perfecting
my awesome hairdo. I looked more like Justin Bieber
than the Bieb himself (four hairstyles ago, that is!).

Then we moved to Bayview and my routine changed,
BIG TIME. I tried heaps of different hobbies. My
parents were desperate for me to feel at home in my new
school and really encouraged me to find my "thing'.

They wanted me to fit in. I guess they were looking out
for me. Or maybe they were just worried that if I was left

to my own devices I might cause another INCIDENT.

Actually that's probably it.

I don't really like to dwell on it, but the INCIDENT is the whole reason my family had to leave the country and move to Bayview in the first place. These days when I think about the INCIDENT my stomach turns. Before the INCIDENT that only happened when Mum served up curried eggs...

So, Mum and Dad talked to Principal Humpton and got me trying every hobby they could think of. I was desperate to make my parents happy—after all, moving to Bayview was ALL MY FAULT—so I went along with it. First up, I visited Lake Bayview to give rowing a go. But, before I even got in the boat I fell into the water. Then I stepped on a yabby.

YEOOOUCH!

So, then Mum suggested that I have a crack at camping. She thought I might feel like I was back home in the bush. But the snarling suburban stray cats really freaked me out. By night they sounded totally like ANGRY HELL BEASTS. Luckily the tent was only pitched in our backyard so I could make a speedy retreat inside.

I also had a go at origami, making animals and flowers from paper. But paper cuts became an issue.

Then I tried karate but kept bumping heads with my opponents as we bowed before each bout. I gave chess a go but I always seemed to get beaten in a handful of moves. Super unlucky I guess.

Dad suggested stamp collecting; no offence but zzzzzzz!

I tried cooking too, but chopping onions made tears stream down my face. Even when I borrowed my sister's swimming goggles I still couldn't stop the flow. Dog walking was no fun either: all the dogs in the neighbourhood wanted to chase me. And after at least a dozen other things I even tried BMX. Which I didn't find X-TREME or even all that X-CITING... Instead I found it simply left me needing X-RAYS.

Usually I'm pretty upbeat, but with all this pressure
to find a hobby I could enjoy problem-free, things were
getting tougher by the day. I was desperate to show
Mum and Dad I was fitting in, and I was super keen
to make up for what I'd done (the INCIDENT).
But no matter how hard I tried I kept failing horribly
at everything.

I had no natural skills!

At anything! Except perfecting my awesome Bieb 'do.

Least of all sport, particularly soccer which seemed
a strange game to me. I'd actually tried out for the
school team pretty soon after we arrived but I couldn't
get my head around why anybody could enjoy playing
a game in which you couldn't use your hands; unless you
were the goalkeeper and he needed gloves anyway.
But, given I'd tried all those other hobbies, AND Archie
and his mates were putting on a show especially for us,
AND the whole class was taking part, I figured I had
to give the game another shot.

So, Dash was right to be excited. Picture the most
AWESOME thing you can think of and multiply it
by AMAZING… then add heaps of INCREDIBLE
(plus a dollop of WOW) and that's how super cool
the clinic was.

Hearing the players talk about what it felt like to play for their country gave me tingles. Then they showed us every trick they knew: how to kick left side, right side, how to dribble, how to dodge opponents, how to fire off a pinpoint pass, how to support your teammates, how to use your head for high balls and how to tackle safely. They even showed us a couple of Socceroo set plays, one after taking a corner, the other after a free kick.

Dash asked Archie to show us how to bend the ball in the air, and he did it one way then the other. He made it all look so simple, not like rowing or origami, and the players made it exciting, not like sticking stamps into a dumb folder. (Good one, Dad.)

I started to think that maybe, just maybe, I might like the game after all. Who needs hands when you can perform magical skills with your feet and your head? Watching Archie, who never stopped smiling, made me want to be like him. Or at least try to.

The clinic finished with a practice match. Archie went along the line and picked out two teams, and handed out different coloured guernseys, all marked with his trademark ARCHIETHOMPSON 10. 10 was his number during his years with the Melbourne Victory. I was playing on Jules. When I first met Jules he greeted me with, "Nice to meet *me*" I asked if he meant "nice to meet *you*?" but he didn't. You don't forget Jules easily. He makes sure of it. And he's a bit of a talker. Actually, he's a lot of a talker.

Archie was the referee, and when he blew the whistle the game was on.

Soon the ball spilt over to me, and I was in the clear. Jules was too distracted discussing the position on the team he'd end up playing when he became a Socceroo. For him, it was a certainty.

I knocked the ball forward just as Archie had showed us, and started running with the ball at my feet, leaving Jules far behind. Suddenly I felt supercharged. My whole body was BUZZING. I ran and ran, then zeroed in on the goals straight ahead. Should I kick with the top of my foot? The side? Both? Or maybe with my left? Will I bend it like Archie?

I closed my eyes. I held my breath. I had NO IDEA what I was doing!

So I stopped thinking and just booted that ball with everything I had.

GOOOOOOOOAL!

Before I could work out how I'd done it, suddenly it was stacks-on Rufus! I've got to say, having a half

a dozen kids jump on me struck me as a pretty strange way to celebrate. But hey, everyone seemed to enjoy it. Including me.

"Rufus," yelled Dash, "You're a star!"

Somehow I'd kicked a goal. Me! For the first time ever I felt like a hero.

"What's your name, kid?" asked Archie, as he helped me to my feet.

"Rufus.' I said.

"Well, from now on, you'll be known as *SOCCERufus*!'

Everybody cheered. I did a little dance on the spot. Principal Humpton chuckled and wobbled.

"Your school must love having you on their soccer team!' said Archie.

"Rufus isn't on the t-t-team." Dash cried, "But he should be!" She started jumping up and down clearly excited by the idea, her fiery red hair flying all about. Suddenly she didn't seem shy at all. "We could use all the help we can get!"

"Sign him up. He's the man!" said Archie.

The other kids gave me the thumbs up. They seemed to love the idea, especially those on the team.

I gave them all a big grin. They were being super

nice. Particularly Dash. I used to be a fairly smiley person, like Archie, but I'm sorry to say that right at that moment I was wearing the kind of smile you make when your auntie gives you boring old socks for Christmas.... FAKE.

I would've loved to be able to help them out. And I really wanted to believe that finally, *finally*, I'd found my 'thing': SOCCER!

But deep down I knew there was one BIG problem.

2

THE BAYVIEW BULLFROGS

Before Archie and the Socceroos left the field, we all gave them three cheers. Actually, because our school soccer team's mascot is a bullfrog, the soccer kids gave them three RIDDUPS!

Riddup! Hooray! Riddup! Hooray! Riddup! Hooray!

I'm sure Archie was impressed. But, come to think of it, he and the Socceroos did disappear pretty quickly after that. I suppose the Aussie players had to prepare for that night's big game that they'd been talking about. Sounded EXCITING.

I've got to be honest, I'd heard the Bayview Bullfrogs weren't much of a team. But I didn't want to be too quick to believe it. However, last year's team photo, that was displayed on the school notice board, didn't exactly make them look like championship-winning material. And the handwriting scribbled beside each player wasn't too positive either. Except for the stuff about the school tough-nuts, the Turner Twins. Strange that.

Coach Wentworth and Principal Humpton gathered the Bullfrogs in front of the clubrooms. Only a handful of the Grade 5s weren't on the school soccer team. I was one of them. My soccer try-out from a few weeks back had been a big FAIL. And training hadn't seemed like much fun… UNTIL TODAY.

THE BAYVIEW

It was lunchtime, so I headed straight for the tuckshop. I'd never kicked a goal before, or come close to anything like it, so I was keen to celebrate with a king size sausage roll with extra sauce. My favourite. Even though I sometimes find those little squeezy sauce packs SUPER tricky.

SQUEEELCH!

But Principal Humpton called me over to the group too. "Rufus Rogers," he said. "Join us for a minute. That was a terrific goal you scored, young man."

I smiled. Something I hadn't been doing much of lately.

Coach Wentworth was happy too. He was rubbing his hands together as he eyed off the many items the Socceroos had signed, all laid out on a Socceroos rug— caps, posters, boots and even Archie's mouthguard— which was still gooey.

"Well, Bullfrogs, what a day! Certainly not one *I'll* forget in a hurry." said Coach Wentworth. "Not only as your coach but also as the acting vice-president of the State Soccer Historians Society! What a collection!"

Principal Humpton laughed and gave a little clap. "Yes, it's been very exciting for all of us."

"I think I'll hang Archie's mouthguard beside the pair of Messi's socks I bought online.' continued Coach Wentworth, pointing inside the clubrooms. "The air will be filled with the scent of talent. A world record holder and the world's greatest, side by side!"

"Dude, if talent smells like that, Stinkin' Lincoln is sure to be a soccer superstar one day!" Jules whispered to me.

I couldn't help laughing. Jules was right. In the short time I'd known Lincoln I'd learnt that although he may have been a whiz at burping the alphabet he was definitely NOT a whiz at taking a shower. Also, it occurred to me that this was the first time I'd ever heard Jules use the term *superstar* to describe anyone but himself.

"Did I hear that right? Why does Coach Wentworth have messy socks? Wouldn't he prefer clean ones?" I whispered to Jules.

"Dude, you're not much of a soccer fan are you?" said Jules. "Don't worry I know everything there is to know. Wentworth is talking about *Leo* Messi – the Barcelona superstar!"

"Oh. Sorry. He sounds pretty cool."

"He is. Y'know a lot of people reckon I play just like Messi.' said Jules, nodding to himself. "Only I'm better of course."

Principal Humpton suddenly turned his attention to me. "So, Rufus, we all want to know how you did it. What a great goal."

"Did you mean to curve the ball through the air..." interrupted Tim Turner.

"...Or was it the wind?" continued Todd Turner. (The Turner Twins often finished each other's sentences. It was freaky.)

"Um." I said. Which wasn't very convincing.

Dash helped me out. "Nice one, Rufus. Smart players know how to use the game's conditions to their advantage," she said. Her face turned red. The sour looks coming from the Turner Twins showed they weren't enjoying Dash's new found confidence. Either that or both of them had their undies on WAY TOO TIGHT.

"Um, thanks Dash." I said.

"It's true though." said Jules, puffing out his chest. "I once scored a goal using the breeze from a flock of geese, a minor earth tremor and a series of rebounds off three large centipedes."

"What? Oh dear me!' cried Coach Wentworth. "The Socceroos forgot to sign my Aussie hankie!"

"Not to worry, Richard," said Principal Humpton. "You have a good collection regardless. Now, boys and girls, after that exciting clinic, I hope we're all feeling inspired for tomorrow morning's first match of the season! Kick off at 11 o'clock!"

"Yeah! Woo-hoo!' The Bullfrogs cheered, still pumped up from the clinic.

"Oh yes. For sure." Coach Wentworth added.

"And young Rufus, I think your parents will be so pleased you've embraced soccer," said the Principal.

"That I've what?" I said.

"I agree with Archie," continued Principal Humpton, "you'd really boost the Bullfrog's chances. Will you join our school team, *Soccerufus*?"

"Him?" said Coach Wentworth.

"Seriously?" I said.

"Seriously!" chuckled the Principal. "And I noticed you were one of the only kids not to get an autograph. So why don't you take this signed Socceroos cap as a memento of the day you became a Bullfrog!"

Principal Humpton picked up one of the many signed caps on the rug but Coach Wentworth grabbed it to stop him.

"That would be okay, wouldn't it, Coach?' said Principal Humpton as they both tugged at the cap.

"Um, *certainly*.' said Coach Wentworth, his eyes bulging. "If he *really* wants it. Do you *really* want it, Rodney?"

"Ah, coach, it's Rufus," I said.

"Wow." whispered Jules. "I never thought I'd see old Wentworth give away some of his precious souvenirs."

It seemed like everyone was looking at me, not just the team, but every kid in the schoolyard AND I wouldn't have been surprised if spy satellites in space were zeroing in on us, as the Principal finally grabbed the cap and held it out for me.

"Um…" I said.

Dash nodded furiously, willing me to take the cap.

"Sorry, but I can't." I said, in a tiny little voice.

Everyone gasped. So much so, it was lucky we were outside the clubrooms and not in them, or we might have had a serious oxygen supply problem.

But as I began to gesture 'no' with an open palm, Principal Humpton must have thought I was accepting the cap. He let it go. I swiped at it, trying to catch it, but I only managed to knock it straight into a puddle of mud. I couldn't believe what I was seeing.

Coach Wentworth dropped to his knees, gurgling. "What just happened?"

"I think what just happened was…"

"…that Rufus was saying he doesn't want to be a Bullfrog." said the Turner Twins. "Oh well."

"That's right. Sorry, but I don't want to join the team." I said, a little louder. (I also didn't want to wear a cap that might hide my great hair, but that seemed a little beside the point right now.)

"Oh. I see." said Principal Humpton.

"That's that then." said Coach Wentworth, storming into the clubrooms with his bundle of Socceroos gear.

Jules scratched his head. Dash looked at her feet. Izzy cracked her knuckles. Happy Hughes looked sadder than ever. And even Stinkin' Lincoln stopped picking his nose for a second to stare at me.

"Um, okay then. I'd better grab some lunch." I said, running off.

"Hey dude, you could be nearly as good as me one day." said Jules, catching up. "What's the deal?"

It was nice of Jules to care, given we didn't know each other that well.

I decided to be straight up with him. "The Turner Twins were right. I fluked the shot. Kicking the goal was awesome but until then I'd stuffed up pretty much everything. There's no use kidding myself, soccer is

simply another fail on my list of hobbies. Every time
I try something new it just ends up going totally wrong."

"Dude, don't overthink everything."

"Nuh. I'm serious. I don't belong on the team.
Trust me, it would only end in disaster."

3

WOWEE, MUM!

I got lost walking home again.

Lucky Bayview is a nice enough place to get lost in. It's got STACKS OF PEOPLE buzzing about—no idea what they're all up to—there's a huge lake in the middle and there's also a little hill where you'll find the school and some shops. In fact I think there could be two hills. Maybe that's where I went wrong. There's definitely only one lake. I'm almost 100% sure of that. I think.

My mind wandered as I passed tiny house after tiny house, finding my way home. Our family would get used to living like battery hens, eventually. Things sure had changed since leaving Biggins Valley. Mum and

Dad used to work together to take care of the farm and the house stuff. But I used to help too, because Dad struggled with the washing just as much as Mum struggled with the shearing.

Hanging around the farm used to be my hobby back then. We were miles away from any other kids or shops or people, even. But mucking around by the creek was super fun.

Suddenly it sunk in that I'd probably never visit the creek again and my insides deflated like a balloon. The farm had been sold. And it was all my fault... thanks to the INCIDENT.

Once I arrived home, I ran straight out the back door to tell Dad and my sisters about the killer goal I'd nailed at the Socceroo clinic. I was about to give a breakdown of every little detail until I realised Dad was totally freaking out.

"It's great to see that old Rufus smile back, mate," he said, as he struggled to get the washing off the line. "But I don't really know all that much about soccer and I'm a little under the pump here."

Mum wasn't home yet. Soon after arriving at Bayview, she'd returned to work as a 'high-flying lawyer'. At least that was how Dad described it.

But as far as I could tell there wasn't all that much flying involved. Just a lot of tapping on her laptop at all hours of the day. Apparently she'd had a similar job before she met Dad. Then me and the girls came along and the farm and family became Mum's thing.

"Nooooo!'" squealed my four-year-old sister Rikki, from the trampoline. My two-year-old sister Ruby had yanked my old teddy, Mr Twinkle, off her. Then the crying started. Both girls. FULL BORE. This wasn't unusual. I'd be lucky not to be deaf before high school.

"Just give me a sec, you two." Dad was battling with a sheet blowing in the wind. Somehow it had wrapped itself around his head like an enormous turban. Even though he still wore flannelette shirts, paint speckled jeans and Blundstones, there wasn't all that much outdoorsy work required at our new place. And looking after the girls on his own all day seemed to be wearing him out more than any job on the farm ever did. Last week, on the way out the door, I yelled 'have a good day', and he simply replied, "Mate, I just aim to get through to dinner time without the house collapsing."

It's fair to say things have changed for Dad. I used to wonder where I got my clumsiness from. Not anymore. Not that I could blame him for struggling. He'd gone from running a farm to working out the twelve different modes on our whizz-bang dishwasher.

I gave Rikki Mr Twinkles and she stopped screaming. But she was a mess. Sometimes I wondered if she was 99% snot. Beside her, little Ruby started laughing as Dad got more and more tangled in the sheet.

Slam! That was the front door closing. Mum was home from her big new job.

"She's early!" Dad cried, now with the sheet completely wrapped around him. He looked like a ghost.

He tripped and landed in the sandpit with a THUD.
Sand flew everywhere. I ran to untangle him.

"Hello everyone!' said Mum looking sharp in her new
business suit.

"Having a little trouble with the washing, you two?'
Mum asked as she dumped her laptop, phone, iPad,
diary, ID pass, document wallet, handbag and keys on
the deck to cuddle the girls.

"All under control, dear.' said ghost-Dad, busily
scraping sand from his hair. The sheet would need to
go through the wash again.

"And is that our dinner smoking away in the oven?'
asked Mum. "Or do we suddenly have a wood fire again?'

"No, that'd be our dinner.' said Dad as he flung the
sheet in my direction and started running inside.
"Hope everyone likes their meat well done."

"Dinner! Dinner!" cried the girls as they chased after
Dad.

"How was your day, Rufus? Finding your way here?'
asked Mum, with a raised eyebrow. She'd asked me this
same question every day since we'd moved to Bayview.

"Oh, young Rufus had a very good day, dear." Dad
called from the kitchen. "He kicked the winning goal in
front of the Soccer-roosters!'

"Not Soccer-roosters, Dad." I corrected him. "Socce*roos*."

"Well that's wonderful, Rufus!" said Mum. "I bet all your new friends were really impressed!"

"Totally! They even asked me to join the school soccer team." I blurted out.

"Great!" said Mum. "We'll have to get you some new boots!"

"Oh. Um. Well, actually I told them I didn't want to be on the team."

"Really?" said Mum. She looked disappointed but tried to hide it with a smile. "Well, that's okay. But can I ask why exactly you didn't want to join the team?"

What I wanted to say was that I felt like I was a walking disaster magnet. And if I put myself out there again and tried to play a new sport like soccer, I was worried that AT BEST I'd let down the team and AT WORST I'd cause another INCIDENT. But I didn't really want to remind her of the INCIDENT. So I simply said, "Um. Well, I'm not really sure it's my thing."

"You could *make* it your thing." said Mum. "As you know, we've been hoping you might get into something new here at Bayview."

"That hasn't really worked out though has it?" I said, glumly.

She put her arm around me, "Have you wanted it to? Because it's not like you to give up."

I didn't know what to say to that. Suddenly I had an overwhelming urge to run inside and help Dad salvage dinner.

"Anyway, it must've been exciting to kick the winning goal. There's no feeling quite like it."

"For sure!' I agreed, the moment rushing back to me. "Hang on. How do *you* know how it feels to kick a goal?"

"Well, I played soccer a little in my younger days. My school team won the championship one year. I used to dream about captaining the Matildas."

"Really?" I said, trying hard to imagine MUM playing SOCCER.

"Don't believe me, huh?" said Mum, "Well, I need to blow off some steam. Do you want to see if I've still got it?"

We turned the trampoline on its side and it became a perfect soccer goal. Mum flicked off her work shoes, shook out her new super serious hairdo, grabbed one of Rikki's toy balls and took a shot.

Smack!

"Wowee, Mum!" She had quite a right foot on her.

I took a shot too. I missed the trampoline completely and hit a tree. A bird's nest fell on my head.

"Gee, that's a powerful kick you've got there, Rufus!" said Mum.

I smiled and pulled the messy nest out of my hair. Mum rarely seemed to notice my stuff ups. Particularly *before* I had caused all of us to pack up our lives and move here to the suburbs. That's what makes a good mum I reckon. That and the ability to cook a killer *spag bol*.

"Would you like a few pointers on ball control?" she asked.

I nodded.

"No problem. When I'm through with you, you'll be dribbling better than Ruby."

We kept up the practice until Mum's mobile phone started ringing. She checked the screen. "It's Principal Humpton...Hello?"

I swallowed. Even though I liked Humpty, ever since the INCIDENT I've found it's usually not a good thing when a school Principal rings your parents.

Mum covered the phone. "He says some of the soccer kids are going to the Socceroos game tonight with Coach Wentworth. They have a spare ticket. He wants to know if you'd like to join them."

I pulled a face.

"Wonderful. He'll be there for sure. We'll leave right away."

Maybe I should've pulled even more of a face.

She hung up. "I'm sure you'll have *tremendous* fun, and I'll be able to pick up some dinner for the family on the way back. I think your Dad has cremated the roast beef."

Uh-oh. I was about to hang out with a whole bunch

of kids who were majorly miffed with me. Maybe that was Mum's idea of *tremendous* fun, but it certainly wasn't mine.

4

RUNNING HARD

It was weird to think Mum could just drop me off at the game. In the country we couldn't just be *dropped off* anywhere. It's a huge deal to go places when you're an hour from the nearest petrol station.

As we drove, Mum explained that tonight's match was a 'friendly' between Australia and Ireland. *Friendly*. Sounded totally chilled. I liked to think that meant all the players would be just sitting around telling jokes over a few milkshakes. But I suppose that probably wouldn't get the fans to fill the grandstands.

The stadium was GINORMOUS. It made the hairs stand up on the back of my neck. I'd never watched much live sport before. Unless you count the sack race at last week's school fair. And I'd rather not. Principal Humpton lost control of his sack and suddenly we all found ourselves in a scene from one of Dad's old Indiana Jones movies.

The grounds outside the stadium were crazy busy. It was noisy and sweaty and there was green and gold everywhere. Everywhere except on me. I'd worn red. At least that's what I'd told myself but since Dad had washed my t-shirt some might say it was closer to pink. With stains that looked like love hearts. No biggie... Right? WRONG.

I'd never seen my Dad struggle at anything quite

so much before. One of my earliest memories was of holding hands with him. Actually it was more like me wrapping my five little fingers around his big index finger. It felt rough and warm but mostly I remember it seemed like it belonged to a giant. I'd wondered if I'd ever grow to be Dad's size.

I was three or four at the time. We'd been walking along the dirt track to the sheep paddocks. I'd been struggling to avoid getting my gumboots stuck in the mud. He'd lifted me over the tricky parts with just his finger. And I remember asking him, "How did you get so good at being a farmer, Dad?"

"Practice." He'd said with a smile. "I made plenty of blues early on, son. But everything comes down to practice."

That was certainly true when it came to my hairstyling. These days I was NAILING IT. But until Dad gets in enough practice to master doing the washing, I'd need to deal with pink t-shirts dotted with love hearts.

It wasn't all Aussies at the game; there were a few Irish fans as well. A group of them were dressed as leprechauns. "Three wishes if you can catch us!" One of them yelled as they rushed past me.

I just needed one wish: to go back in time. How I'd love to be able to change the past so that the INCIDENT never happened.

I actually dreamt about that the night before. In my dream I'd stepped into a weird glowing time portal, wearing a fake beard and sunnies to ensure that I didn't freak out my younger self. My plan was to warn myself before I missed the bus that day and everything went so wrong. But in the dream I went too far back in time and ended up being chased by dinosaurs. (Mental note: lay off the cheese before bed—causes serious nightmares).

The atmosphere outside the ground was something else. As I approached our meeting point, I was considering trying to stick some of the free 'Go Aussie' stickers they were handing out over the hearts on my t-shirt when I heard familiar voices.

"Well, well, look who we have here…'

"…if it isn't *Soccerufus* himself!' said the Turner Twins.

"Oh. Hi." I said.

Fortunately, the Twins were not alone: Jules, Dash, Izzy, Llama, Stinkin' Lincoln and the Karate Kevins were there too. None of them seemed all that thrilled to see me. In fact it looked like they were about to tell me to NICK OFF.

Coach Wentworth was nearby taking photos. He also gave me a dirty look. He was probably still upset about the muddy cap.

"Why are you…"

"…wearing bright *pink*?" asked the Turner Twins.

"It's red." I replied.

"With love hearts?" the Twins sniggered.

"Real men wear p-p-pink." said Dash. "That's what my Dad says."

"That's true. I wear pink sometimes." said Jules, nodding to himself. "As a matter of fact, I wear pink undies all the time."

Izzy gave Jules a weird look. Fair enough. Jules just kept nodding. I was starting to think there was something wrong with his neck.

"Plenty of time until the game starts." said Llama. "Before all the parked cars fill up this section, we should have a kick."

A kick? Gee. This time of day in Biggins Valley used to mean helping Mum read bedtime stories to Ruby and Rikki, while Dad checked the stables. Now, I was playing soccer with a bunch of kids I didn't really know before attending an international sporting event.

Was this smart?

I glanced around and lost count of how many catastrophes I might be able to cause in a place like this.

I should have stayed at home. It's just that the whole soccer thing seemed to impress Mum. But then again, Ruby eating her breakfast without getting Weet-Bix in her hair also got Mum pretty pumped. Still, I'd do practically anything if it meant that one day they'd forgive me for the INCIDENT.

Maybe even risk another one?

"Better idea…"

"…let's play five on five." said the Turner Twins.

"Only if I'm on Rufus' team." said Dash, grabbing a ball from her backpack. "I want to see some of his *other* tricks."

I laughed.

But I was the only one.

Maybe she wasn't joking.

"Fine, we'll take Izzy," said the Turner Twins as Jules began striding towards the Twins' team, expecting to be picked. "And the Karate Kevins. Best of a bad bunch."

Jules didn't know which way to turn.

"You're on *our* team, hotshot." said Llama, passing the ball around to warm up.

"Now Jules," said Llama, "Try not to get tackled straight away like you always do."

"Sounds like the *captain* can't handle being shown up. Is that why you hog the ball?" Jules replied.

Stinkin' Lincoln burped. "You both suck."

"Is that really how you guys speak to each other?" I said, without thinking.

"Yep, why?" said Llama.

"Nothing. Well, almost nothing. I mean, look, as teammates maybe you should try to be a bit more *positive*?" I suggested, thinking that might help.

Jules gritted his teeth. Dash mouthed "ooooh'. They were right: it wasn't really my place to give advice to the Bullfrogs captain. But Llama simply shrugged.

A TV crew were nearby, getting shots of the crowd. The cameraman was halfway up a tree, trying to get a high shot of all the action.

"Hey, Mr Cameraman, get some footage of this kid." yelled Todd Turner.

"Yeah, he thinks he's the next Archie Thompson. Calls himself *Soccerufus*!' laughed Tim Turner.

"The kid in pink?" asked the cameraman. "With the love hearts?"

"That's him!" said Jules. He gave me a thumbs up,

like he thought he was being helpful to me. "But Mr Cameraman, you'll probably want to record a few of *my* highlights first. I'm even *better* than Archie ever was!"

But the cameraman pointed his lens directly at me. NO PRESSURE.

We took our positions and Dash kicked off. She flicked the ball out to Jules. Todd Turner swooped in to try and tackle him. Jules could see Todd Turner coming and started to hesitate.

"You can do it, Jules." cried Llama.

This seemed to help, because just in time, Jules focussed and flicked the ball out wide, half a second before Todd Turner reached him. Llama took the pass not far from me.

"Positivity, huh? Soccerufus, you might not be as dumb as you look." said Llama.

Huh? She thought I looked dumb? Hadn't she seen my hair?

But before I could come up with a super smart comment she passed me the ball. Suddenly one of the Karate Kevins was coming for me. I tapped the ball forward along the imaginary wing. Total accident but it looked like I was dribbling. That's right: me!

The tall Karate Kevin was hot on my heels. My mind

raced as I ran along behind the ball. But it felt great to be playing my part. Suddenly I had teammates, and maybe, maybe, I was beginning to make *friends*?

I pushed the thought of disaster out of my mind, I was having TOO MUCH FUN TO WORRY. I sped along, using a handy hint or two that Mum had shared in the backyard about ball control. *Gentle contact. Keep the ball close. Use your body to protect it.* And it was actually working!

Then suddenly the two big trees were right there. They were the goals.

I got the same BUZZ again that I'd had that morning at the clinic. It was a feeling like nothing else; the ball at your feet, rushing past the world with a target in your sights. PURE ADRENALIN.

My teammates were yelling but I blocked it all out. I was determined to score another awesome goal. I didn't worry too much about how to kick the ball, I just thumped it with everything I had.

SMACK!

I fell flat on my bum. The ball went straight up into the air. Then bopped me on the head.

'Oooof!'

"Ha! Looks like Soccerufus reckons he's Besart Berisha..."

"...crossed with Bruno Fornaroli!" laughed the Turner Twins.

I started rubbing my backside, "Um. I'm not really sure what that means..."

"Rufus! Why didn't you cross it to Dash? She was wide open." asked Llama.

"It's c-c-cool," said Dash, running over. "You okay?"

"Sorry, stuffed it up."

"That's okay," said Dash. "It was a great run along the wing."

"Really? I guess it was, wasn't it?" I smiled. Up until the moment I totally screwed up the shot, I was having a total blast.

"Chop chop!" called Coach Wentworth. "We can't afford to dilly-dally otherwise someone might grab our seats."

"Better get moving." said Dash helping me up off the grass, "We *really* don't want to get on Coach Wentworth's b-b-bad side..."

Then Dash put her hand to her mouth, as if she'd misspoke. "I mean..."

"I know what you mean." I said. "And yes, I noticed he wasn't exactly stoked after I dropped his special cap in the mud this morning."

"Hey, what do you care?" said Jules. "You don't want to be a Bullfrog anyway."

"True." I said.

But why didn't it *feel* true anymore? Did part of me actually want to give soccer a proper go, now? If so, I'd need to win back Coach Wentworth somehow. But actually playing was a huge step up from a clinic. Was I really considering putting myself out there in such a way again? Wouldn't that be asking for disaster? Again.

Jules pushed me towards the entrance. "Come on, slow coach."

As we headed into the stadium, Todd Turner cried out to the cameraman who was packing up his gear. "Hey Camera Guy, that footage you just shot, what channel will that be on? We'd love to record it!"

"No channel. This is footage for the big screen inside.' said the cameraman. "We'll be playing it before the match."

My heart SUNK. In fact I think it probably dropped down to somewhere near my feet. 50,000 people were about to see me fall smack on my bum. Probably with some hilarious sound effects.

"Come on Bullfrogs!' cried Tim Turner, speeding

everyone up through the turnstiles. "We don't want to miss the Soccerufus show on the big screen!"

"No." I muttered as we ran up a set of stairs. "Wouldn't want to miss that."

5

THE BIG SCREEN

I struggled to keep up with the others as we searched for our seats. There was a mass of people inside the stadium and I had to zig and zag through the crowd. It felt like I was in a maze. One wrong turn and I was sure to be lost forever. It reminded me of the time that Dad and I got trapped in a hedge maze out in the country. Things got so bad that Dad took off his boxer shorts and wrote HELP on them, before waving them around on a stick for attention. (The boxers were the brightest material he had, by the way. But at least his undies weren't pink like Jules'.)

Pity a seagull stole them, and then dropped them on a security guard who was less than impressed.

Once Coach Wentworth finally found our seats we

were forced to struggle past a guy wearing a watermelon for a hat, a kid in a kangaroo costume and another dude we thought had dressed as a leprechaun; green suit, fluffy beard and all. (Jules playfully yanked on the guy's beard. "Yeow," he shouted. Turned out he wasn't in costume. We all learned a lesson there.)

The soccer pitch below glistened under the stadium lights. I slotted in between Dash and Jules. We had good seats. Actually we had great seats. The only way we could have had better seats was if we'd been on the Aussie substitution bench. And seeing it all before me, I had to admit, part of me wished that I was on that bench; or even better on the field. Imagine being an actual Socceroo! Striding towards goal in the mighty green and gold, representing my country. My heart skipped a beat just thinking about it.

"Dude, what's wrong with you?" asked Jules, waving his hand in front of my face. "You're grinning like you've just fallen in love or something."

"Sorry." I said. But maybe Jules was right. Despite knowing it was probably a bad idea, I think I *was* falling in love—WITH SOCCER!

"The love heart t-shirt's gone to his head!" laughed Tim Turner.

The Turner Twins had their eyes glued to the big screen, waiting for my 'highlights' to be shown. It's possible the twins might have actually forgotten there was a game on at all. "I can't wait to see the *big* fall on the *big* screen," said Todd Turner.

"Try not to think about it, Rufus." said Dash. "Just concentrate on the great run you had *before* your little muck up. You looked like you were loving it!"

That bit *had* been fun. And I hadn't really been having much of that lately. For a moment I'd felt like my old self again.

"Maybe joining the Bullfrogs might be more enjoyable than you think?" Dash added, softly. I could tell she was trying to lift my spirits without bugging me to change my decision.

"Maybe." I said. And I think she believed she might be getting somewhere. I certainly wasn't worried about letting them down any more. I may not have been a soccer superstar just yet, but that didn't really matter. It was fun either way, and it was nice to know that at least one of the Bullfrogs wanted me on the team.

"Dude, you're drooling." said Jules.

I was about to apologise when a voice came over the speakers. "Good evening ladies and gentlemen and welcome to tonight's friendly International Match between Australia and Ireland. Who's supporting the Socceroos?"

The crowd roared.

I spotted the announcer in the centre of the pitch, grinning from ear to ear. "Great to hear it! And is there anyone here going for the Irish?'

A *much* quieter cheer.

"There's a few... *To be sure, to be sure!* Ha ha ha!"

"I don't get it." said Stinkin' Lincoln.

"How do you make an Irish stew?" asked the announcer.

"You make him watch his team lose to the Aussies!"

The Socceroos fans cheered, but it was almost drowned out by the sound of the announcer laughing into his microphone. He obviously thought he was a world-class comedian.

"I don't get that either," said Stinkin' Lincoln.

"Now, ladies and gentlemen," said the announcer, finally getting serious. "We've had a cameraman filming you all as you arrived tonight. So, if you're lucky, you might get to see yourself on the big screen!"

"Uh-oh." I muttered, sinking down into my seat. "Here we go."

I glimpsed the Turner Twins smirking at me. Not in a friendly way. More like crocodiles.

"Dude, they'd better show some footage of *me*." said Jules. "The selectors will sign me up on the spot."

The announcer continued. "All eyes on the big screen!"

The footage started. It showed a man dressed as a green and gold ninja, karate chopping at the camera as he made his way into the stadium.

"Wow! That's our instructor, Derek!" muttered the taller Karate Kevin. I recognised him too, from my failed attempt at learning karate a few weeks back.

Then the screen showed a granny in a motorised

scooter. She blew the crowd a kiss and her false teeth fell out. Everyone laughed, which made her very grumpy.

I whispered to Dash, "The biggest joke is still to come."

"It might not be as b-b-bad as you think." said Dash, trying to be nice.

"Here we go, *Soccerufus*!" sniggered Tom Turner.

Then the footage of me came up on screen. I peeked through my fingers. At least my hair looked good.
I was running along dribbling the ball. Dash was right, I looked super-pumped. The crowd cheered. And then the screen cut to a Socceroos logo.

"What?" I said.

"WHAT?" shouted both the Turner Twins, standing up in their seats.

The bit where I fell over wasn't shown!

"Is that all they're going to play?" I asked Jules, hoping it was true.

"Better not be, dude! I did some *amazing* stuff and they didn't show one second."

The announcer continued, "Now, the three soccer fans who were just shown on the screen have each been selected to compete in the half-time penalty challenge!"

"In the what?" I said.

"So you three had better start channelling your inner Archie Thompson and Tim Cahill and Mile Jedinak, all rolled into one because you'll need to score from the penalty line to win a signed Socceroos Jumper! Good luck! See you down here at half-time!'

"Awesome, Rufus!" said Dash. "You'll totally smash this!"

"Wow, you'll give me the jumper if you win, right?" said Jules. "Y'know, after you kick for goal in front of a full house."

The Turner Twins laughed. "Yeah right! As if he'll win!"

Izzy sighed so loudly at their antics that she almost blew her snacks over the balcony.

"This is massive!" said Llama.

"Sorry, Rufus" said the shorter Karate Kevin. "But we're going for Derek."

I shrugged. It was all I could manage as blind panic had set in. I started grinning like a maniac.

"What's better than watching Soccerufus stuff up on the big screen?" asked Todd Turner.

"I know. Watching him stuff up LIVE!" laughed Tim Turner.

"Look, we all know they should've picked me to be in

the comp," said Jules. "But I guess I can give you a few pointers before you line up."

Suddenly Stinkin' Lincoln worked out what was going on. "Oh, *you're* taking a penalty shot, Rufus? Whoa. Pretty sick, huh?"

"Yeah." I agreed. Sick was right. But he probably meant 'sick' as in *awesome*. I meant it in the so-nervous-you're-about-to-spew-your-whole-guts-up sort of way...

My heart was thumping against my chest like a jackhammer. This had the potential to turn out even worse than the INCIDENT.

6

FROZEN

I don't remember the national anthem being sung. I don't remember the first half of the game. I just barely remember the watermelon flying off the head of the guy behind us...

Mainly because of its landing...

But I do remember the words that came up on the screen at around the 40th minute. The message asked the penalty challenge competition winners to head to a meeting point behind the players' bench. I didn't move. Instead I just kept cheering on the Socceroos hoping my classmates didn't notice the screen.

"Check out the big screen..."

"...It's your starring moment, Soccerufus!" yelled the Turner Twins.

I began to tremble. Was it too late to hide under the seat?

"This is s-s-so exciting, Rufus." said Dash. "Congratulations again!"

"Um, yeah." I said, through clenched teeth. This whole turn of events was really starting to test my newfound love of soccer. And it was also starting to test my bowel control too, to be honest.

"Have you ever..."

"...Actually taken a penalty shot before?" asked the Turner Twins. But they laughed straight after, so I guess they knew the answer. (For the record, the answer's a big NO.)

There'd been a penalty shot in the Socceroos game a few minutes earlier. A hush had fallen around the stadium. (Except when I sneezed.) Everyone was on the edge of their seats. I got sweaty palms just watching. What made it worse was the shot hit the crossbar. The goal keeper didn't need to do a thing to make the save. If a professional player couldn't score a penalty, what chance would *I* have?

"Dude, you could be the next Ronaldo," said Jules.

"Ronaldo MacDonald?" I asked, not thinking straight. "What's the clown from Maccas got to do with it? And how can he kick with those massive red and yellow shoes?"

"No, you nutcase, *Christiano* Ronaldo. He plays for Real Madrid. Awesome penalty record."

"Look, Jules, I'm not sure I can do this.' I said. "If I can't hide under my seat, can you smuggle me into the toilets?"

"What?" said Jules. "Don't you want to be a soccer superstar? You were pumped about kicking that goal in Archie's clinic this morning, weren't you?"

"Well, yeah."

"So, go do it again. Simple."

"Simple? I'm not so sure about that."

"There is one *other* good reason to give this a go." said Dash. "If you win the signed jumper and present it to Coach Wentworth, he might forgive you and invite you back on the Bullfrogs team."

I hadn't thought of that. I hadn't thought of anything much beyond EMBARRASSMENT ON A WORLD-WIDE SCALE.

But Dash was right. If I wanted to play for the Bullfrogs—and I was starting to think that maybe I did—I needed to get back on Coach Wentworth's good side. And winning him over with some signed memorabilia was the perfect way to do it.

"You could be right." I said and I got to my feet, intending to call out across the row to Coach Wentworth to see if he was keen on the jumper, but his seat was empty. Big mistake. The crowd around me recognised my face from the screen and they started cheering.

Then Jules got them chanting.

SOCCERUFUS! CLAP-CLAP-CLAP!
SOCCERUFUS! CLAP-CLAP-CLAP!

"Now, you *have* to go, dude!" said Jules, and he gave me a big thumbs up.

Dash shrugged. Further along the row, Izzy glared at me, clearly not impressed with my uncertainty. The Karate Kevins used karate chop stances to silently warn me not to beat their teacher and the Turner Twins were making cry baby gestures. At least Stinkin' Lincoln was ignoring me; he was too impressed by a chunk of wax he'd pulled from his ear.

I flicked the watermelon seeds out of my hair—if I was going to be the centre of attention I at least wanted my 'do to look its best—and I started walking to the meeting point. Every step I took it felt like my knees were going to give way. I was sure I could hear the Turner Twins laughing the whole time.

I stood alongside the other competition winners just inside the fence. Derek, the martial arts teacher, bowed at me. "We meet again." I didn't bow back because when I gave his karate class a go I found that I had a strange tendency to clash heads in such situations.

Before I could say hello to the granny, she reversed her scooter over my foot. It must have been an accident. I'm sure she wasn't as grumpy as she looked and I'm certain she would have apologised if the crowd hadn't been so loud.

Then the referee whistled to signal half-time. The score was nil all. As each team left the field, a security guard walked the three of us out to the penalty box. (BTW, it took me a few seconds to work out what that was. When I first heard the term *penalty box* I had assumed it was some kind of medieval torture.)

Being on the field was way different from being in the stands. We were SURROUNDED. Masses of people loomed over us. I blinked a few times into the blinding lights. Right about now, fainting seemed my best option.

The announcer came over to us, and introduced us to the crowd. "...we have a nanna, a ninja and a nincompoop!"

Laughs. 50,000 of them. I caught a glimpse of myself on the big screen. I was grinning like a maniac.
And I'd gone bright red.

"Just kidding!" continued the announcer, who'd massively overdone his after shave. "I LOVE the pink t-shirt *and* the hearts, kid!'

I was so wound up I'd forgotten what I was wearing. Probably a good thing.

"So what's your name, young fella?"

"Rufus"

"Dufus?"

More laughs.

"Roooo-fus.' I said, miffed he was embarrassing me before I even had a chance to try and avoid it, "As in, *Soccerufus*!"

As soon as I said it I wished I could take it back. There was no point explaining anything by using my new nickname; no one in the crowd knew it. Except for my new schoolmates, who immediately started the Soccerufus chant again. Within seconds it swept the whole stadium.

SOCCERUFUS! CLAP-CLAP-CLAP!

SOCCERUFUS! CLAP-CLAP-CLAP!

And then the strangest thing happened.

I liked it.

Sure I was nervous—more than I'd ever been in my entire life—but I was also FULLY PUMPED. I wanted this. Jules was right: I wanted to be a soccer superstar. And the first step to stardom was kicking this goal and winning the signed jumper in front of a packed stadium. It was my ticket to getting on the school soccer team.

It was a bit like when Dad finally admits he wants dessert. Even though every night he makes a big show of being on a diet.

The announcer invited Derek the martial arts instructor to step up to the penalty spot. Derek tried to promote his karate class but the announcer pulled the mic away.

"One shot each. Score a goal and you win the signed jumper." said the announcer. "Good luck Derek, hope you can kick goals as well as you can kick butt!'

Derek didn't take a run up. Instead he stood in a crane stance. As he kicked the ball he yelled, "Hee-ya!"

The ball rocketed off sideways and hit the announcer right in the... Well let's just say he was hit in the HIDDEN DRAGON and went all CROUCHING TIGER.

The crowd went OOOOOOOOOH!

As the announcer got to his feet he demanded the security guards assist Derek straight off the field. Derek yelled out the name of his karate business as he was marched away.

The grumpy granny was quick to get her scooter in position for her kick.

She gave me the stink eye. "Look out, sonny. I've got one good leg and I'm not afraid to give you a good old-fashioned walloping with it.'

I moved aside.

Grumpy Granny took a long run up (or should that be drive up?) and she tried to thump the ball with her right foot. It only moved a few centimetres. She didn't have the power to kick it any further. She attempted another kick. But she drove her cart over the ball and POPPED it.

"Maybe we should give her a closer shot." I suggested.

The announcer seemed like he was about to agree till the old lady blew a raspberry at him.

"Rules are rules! Off you scoot." said the announcer. "It's your turn, Soccerufus!"

The crowd started chanting my name again.

I couldn't stop myself thinking about ALL THE PEOPLE in the stands watching me.

"If you kick this goal, you win the signed Socceroos jumper." As if I needed reminding. It was my key to convincing Coach Wentworth to give me a second chance.

I HAD to kick the goal. My future with the Bullfrogs depended on it. This was my first step to one day becoming a Socceroo. I tried to remember all the tips Archie had given us about kicking for goal: *use the inside of your foot, pick a target and place the ball in the goals. Don't bang it in.*

I ran up to the ball and then...

In an instant I imagined all the ways I could stuff this up. My next move could cause any one of a million different catastrophes in a stadium like this.

I froze. I was paralysed with fear.

7

MOVE IT OR LOSE IT!

I couldn't move. I was frozen stiff in the middle of a packed stadium. My mind was a blur, filled with a MILLION different emotions.

If you could have seen inside my brain, it probably would have been a mad house.

"What's the problem here, young Soccerufus?' Asked the announcer as he slapped me on the back. This caused a reflex action. My leg swung forwards.

THUD!

I kicked the ball.

Nowhere near as hard as I'd wanted to. It landed only half way towards the goals.

"Oooh, *heart* breaking!' laughed the announcer pointing to the heart shapes on my t-shirt. "Bad luck.'

But the crowd started *oohing* and *aahing*. The ball was still rolling. It was drawing closer to the goal line. Lucky I'd got my foot in the position Archie had recommended for taking a penalty shot, so the ball was bang-on target.

I stopped breathing. I shut out everything but the ball. "Roll!" I yelled. "ROLL!"

The ball was moving painfully slow but it was dribbling closer and closer to the goal line. Would it make it?

Not far ahead of the ball, a crow landed. It was standing right in the way. I wondered if it could possibly be the same evil crow from the INCIDENT. Was he back to taunt me? No. He moved aside to avoid the ball.

My whole future depended on a stupid ball crossing a stupid line. "Come on!" I shouted.

A light breeze hit me in the face. Would it stop the ball? Or with the breeze swirling in all directions around the stadium, would it be enough to push the ball across the line?

The announcer was jumping up and down beside me,

commentating for the crowd. Was his stomping helping? I started running on the spot, willing the ball forward.

The ball turned. Painfully slowly. Then, with one last rotation, it stopped...across the line.

"Woo-hoo!' I jumped up into the air. I'd done it! I'd scored another GOOOOOOAL!

The crowd ROARED! And the Soccerufus chant started again. I waved to all the supporters. Then I did a dance. Everyone in the stands copied my little jig. I even gave the announcer a big hug.

"Ooof," he grunted. "Well done, young Soccerufus! I would never have predicted it, but you've turned out to be the winner of the Socceroos signed jumper."

I held the gold guernsey up to the crowd. They chanted my name again. I was a hero. A soccer superstar! And it was AWESOME!

Then suddenly it dawned on me that all this was only temporary. So, right that second I promised myself to do whatever it took to get back here on this very pitch one day and have them cheer for me again. Eventually I would live up to my nickname and be a proper Socceroo!

I was whisked off the field by security. They gave me a special bag for my prized guernsey and walked me back to my seat. Dash jumped up and hugged me. Jules gave me a high five and Izzy raised an eyebrow in a very meaningful way (she must've been impressed). Llama gave me a clap but the Karate Kevins seemed a bit flat. The Turner Twins said nothing.

The second half of the match was super fun. The Socceroos kicked away, winning 6-0. One of the Aussie strikers booted five of the goals.

"Is that some sort of record?' I asked while cheering the Socceroos as they left the pitch.

"Nah. Don't you remember?" said Jules.

"Oh yeah," I said. "Archie Thompson once kicked 13 against American Samoa.'

"Dude, you're actually starting to sound like you're learning a thing or two about soccer!' said Jules.

"Maybe I am.'

"And you'll be able to use all that knowledge when you're p-p-part of the team." said Dash. "Perhaps now is the right time to win back Coach Wentworth with the signed jumper?"

"Whoa!' I cried as Todd Turner swiped the bag containing the jumper from my lap. He threw it to Tim who was already sprinting up the aisle.

"Hey!' said Dash. "Not funny."

Jules laughed. "They're just mucking around."

Izzy stood and grunted.

Todd Turner followed Tim Turner up the stairs. They were disappearing into the crowd.

"They're *so* not mucking around." said Dash. "They've stolen your s-s-signed Socceroos jumper."

Izzy CRACKED her knuckles.

"I've got to get it back!" I cried, leaping the row of seats behind us. "It's my key to getting on the school soccer team!"

I leaped from row to row. Luckily, I was graceful enough

to avoid stepping on anyone. Well, that's not strictly true, but at least I didn't cause serious injury. That I know of.

I chased the Turner Twins up the aisle and through the exit that led to the maze of wide open corridors and stairs behind the grandstand. Luckily there was no easy way down to the main exits. This section of the stadium was all snack shops, merchandising stalls and masses of people. Unfortunately, that was slowing me down too.

Then someone appeared at my side. Dash.

"You're fast."

"Haven't you ever wondered why people call me, Dash?" she winked. "Come on, the Twins are probably heading for the nearest exit, which is Gate 3. If they make it into the car p-p-park then we're no chance of stopping them."

"We can't let that happen." I said.

"Totally. That's why I have Jules on the case." She nodded behind her.

"How's *he* going to help?"

Suddenly fizzy drink SQUIRTED through the air. A stream flew right over the top of us and landed on the people exiting Gate 3. Those about to leave flinched backwards, trying to avoid the sticky spray.

Jules stood up on the snack bar bench like he was an action hero.

"Say hello to my FIZZY friend!" He yelled, moments before security guards yanked the fizzy drink dispenser from his hands.

"There they are! The twins are headed for Gate 2," said Dash, peering through the crowd.

"Come on, come on!" I yelled. "We need to force them back this way."

Past the people to my left, my announcer friend was on his microphone explaining how to leave the stadium. (In between bad gags). "Are there any Irish supporters still here or have they all lepre-GONE! Ha ha ha!"

"Dash, I need to borrow your ball." Before she answered I grabbed it from her backpack and KICKED it. Goal! I hit the announcer in the stomach and the microphone flew from his hands. I dived to retrieve it.

"Ladies and gentlemen!" My voice echoed through the PA. I sounded a little too kid-like so I channelled Batman and talked real low. "The Socceroos are now signing autographs at Gate 2. Everyone welcome!"

INSTANT HUMAN TRAFFIC JAM!

"Nice one! They won't be getting out that way either!" said Dash.

But as I got to my feet the Turner Twins whizzed past us, heading to Gate 4, just as another group of people got in our way.

We were blocked by a wall of supporters, smelly, hot and unbreakable. They didn't seem like people anymore, just a mass of arms and legs that was growing larger and larger by the second, speeding this way and that. And there was no way through.

Darn it! We weren't going to catch the twins. The jumper was as good as theirs. Was my Bullfrog dream over before it began?

8

RUN!

Dash and I raced sideways along the wall of people in our way. The Turner Twins had stolen my signed Socceroos jumper—the key to me getting onto the Bullfrogs team—and we had to stop them leaving the stadium or we may never get it back. We'd caused chaos at the other nearby exits, which meant Gate 4 had to be where the twins were headed. Along with everyone else. As we got closer we saw it was super busy there too.

As we ran I jumped high in the air to try and catch a glimpse of the Turner Twins on the other side of the mass of people.

Nuh.

Nuh.

Yep.

I spotted the twins up ahead, still separated from us by the crowd. Back on the farm if Dad wanted to get a large group of sheep to move he used our sheepdog, Bluey. We needed Bluey now, but he wasn't around anymore and I doubt they would've sold him a ticket to the game anyway. But perhaps we had the next best thing.

"You have a strange look in your eye." said Dash as we ran. "What are you p-p-planning, Rufus?"

"Just get low." I said, then I put the 'borrowed' mic to my mouth once more... And started BARKING LIKE A DOG.

"Woooof! Wooof! Raaaawl! Wooof! Grrrrr!"

The sound was so full on it even made *me* jump. I instantly got flashbacks from my recent dog-walking fiasco. The barking noise came through the speakers sounding more like some kind of hellhound than old Bluey. But it worked.

The crowd slowed for a moment. People seemed confused. They couldn't work out where the noise was coming from. One or two kids started crying. Sorry!

I grabbed Dash's hand and staying low we crawled through the crowd's legs. Then I lost all sense of direction and hit a rubbish bin and its contents spilt all over me. I dropped the mic. The people started moving again the moment the barking stopped.

Suddenly I smelt worse than Stinkin' Lincoln but we'd made it through and I recognised the hairy legs of the Turner Twins just ahead. We got back up on our feet. "Gotcha!"

They grinned at us. "Not yet you haven't."

I SWIPED for the bag but they WHIPPED it out of reach. Several supporters started crossing between us. Dash and I battled though, the last thing we needed was another barrier of bodies in our way.

"Not hiding away with your books tonight, D-d-d-ash. What's got into you?" teased Todd Turner.

"Yeah, we're not sure we l-l-like this *new you*!" said Tim Turner.

Dash went red in the face again. "Maybe Rufus has shown me we don't have to put up with *your* antics to be a Bullfrog." And she didn't stutter a single word.

"Him? He's no Bullfrog."

Suddenly there was an opening as people between us cleared away. We ran at the Turner Twins.

They backed up. A tiny gap in the crowd formed behind them. They'd soon realise that they were able to duck away and disappear. I grabbed for them. They were out of reach. They turned and...

SMACK!

They ran into Izzy.

Before the twins had even realised what happened, Izzy plucked the bag containing the jumper out of their hands and hurled it at me.

Todd Turner forced a laugh. "Go easy! We were going to give it back!"

"Yeah, it was just a joke!" said Tim Turner.

"Hilarious." I said, stepping right up to them, not really sure what I had in mind. I'm totally a peaceful dude after all.

Beep! Beep!

Just then, the grumpy granny ZIPPED between us in her scooter. I was flung backwards. "See ya, suckers!"

Once she'd gone the Turner Twins had disappeared. It didn't really matter, not now that I had the signed Socceroos jumper back. My soccer future was back on track. YEAH!

I was out of breath for a while, but when Jules, Dash and Izzy starting kicking a ball around in the car park, that didn't stop me joining in.

FUN TIMES. I was disappointed when we had to stop playing and pile into Jules' Mum's car to be dropped home.

As I entered the house, Dad was midway through washing a stack of dirty dishes. (He'd given up on the fancy dishwasher.) I grabbed a tea towel and started drying seconds before they all toppled over.

"Oh, hi mate. Thanks. Your mother's busy lawyer-ing on her laptop. She had some crisis or other to attend to." said Dad, wiping his brow and leaving a trail of bubbles on his forehead. "Plus, Rikki keeps getting up. Reckons she can't sleep."

"As long as she doesn't wake Ruby, or we're all in for it." I said.

"You're not wrong." Dad laughed, "So um, how was the footy?"

"Soccer."

"Right. *Soccer*. Fun?"

"Totally, mind-blowingly, unforgettably awesome!"

"Really?' said Dad. He stopped washing dishes and ruffled my hair, sharing the bubbles. "That's great to hear, mate."

I was so pumped that even dirty water on my hairdo didn't seem to annoy me. "I've decided that soccer is pretty darned awesome, Dad. I could've played it all night."

"I'll play! I'll play!" said Rikki, appearing at the bottom of the stairs in her pj's. "But I want to be the vampire!"

"You're meant to be asleep." sighed Dad. "Hang on, what do *vampires* have to do with soccer?"

"Nothing.' I said. "I think she means *umpire*."

"Actually she means *referee*." said Mum, entering the living room. "But some people do think they are monsters, Rikki."

Mum picked her up and made a growling sound. Rikki giggled.

"Let's watch a little soccer on the sports channel. You might find it interesting after tonight, Rufus. But more importantly, it might put Rikki to sleep." said Mum. "You're okay to finish off the dishes, dear?"

"Um, sure thing." said Dad, accidentally SQUIRTING the dishwasher liquid over himself. I was starting to think he and I had a lot more in common than I ever realised.

The three of us sunk into the couch. Mum flicked on a soccer game. It was Manchester United versus Arsenal in the English Premier League. (I know it sounds rude, but honestly, there really is a team called Arsenal).

"I knew you'd have fun tonight." said Mum.

"It was awesome. I even won a signed jumper."

"Really? Nice work!" said Mum. "So, soccer, huh?"

"Yeah." I said. "You might be right. Maybe I could *make* it my thing. I'm not really sure whether I'll be much help to the team though."

And I was still worried about whether or not me playing soccer might somehow cause another INCIDENT. But I didn't feel like bringing that up just then.

"You'll be a great help to the team." said Mum. "Think about back on the farm. Things got hard at times. But you helped your father where you could and me too of course. And you weren't exactly a natural at that either. There were often times we really did rely on you to pull the family together. You stayed positive. You worked hard and most of all you *never gave up*. We needed that... All teams need that."

"Thanks." I said. "But what if I can't remember to do that stuff out on the field?"

"Rufus." said Mum. "That's just who you are."

I caught Mum's MASSIVE SMILE reflected in the TV. That made me happy too.

Rikki leant against me and yawned. I whispered to

Mum, "I might even be playing for the school team
as soon as tomorrow." At least, that was my plan.

"Tomorrow? Wow." She mouthed back. As Rikki
began snoring.

It could've been the glare of the TV but for a moment
I thought that Mum had gone a little misty-eyed.

KERRASHHH!

Uh oh. Dad accidently dropped a plate. Mum raced
over to assist.

But Rikki didn't wake. So, I stood with her in my
arms, letting her head rest on my shoulder. As I carried
her back to her bedroom I crossed my fingers that I'd be
allowed to join the Bullfrogs. I was determined to talk
Coach Wentworth into letting me play in tomorrow's
opening game of the season. Surely the signed Socceroos
jumper would do the trick. I'd soon find out.

9

BANANAS FOR BREAKFAST

I got up SUPER EARLY.

Not because I was excited. Even though I totally was.

I got up early because Rikki fell out of bed and woke the whole house. I knew Rikki wouldn't go back to sleep, so I took her downstairs to play until the sun came up. We pretended her dolls were playing a soccer match.

FYI—Barbie has a killer left foot.

"Ru-ru, when you're older, like eleventeen, would you like to be a soccer player?" Rikki asked.

"Yep. Totally. You?"

"Hmmm. I want to be a pink sparkly thing."

"What a chip off the old block," Dad muttered as he entered the living room. "Who wants brekky?'

After bananas for breakfast—recommended by Manchester United and England soccer star Wayne Rooney, according to my internet search for 'soccer food'—I found my way to Jules' place and he let me borrow some of his boots and a mouthguard he'd never used. (At least he said he'd never used it. I tried not to think about it.)

We walked to school together. I was still getting used to seeing so many people out and about. What were they all doing? Life in the suburbs seemed super busy. And no one ever said *hello*. It was just plain rude.

We walked along passing Jules' soccer ball between us. Jules re-enacted some of the previous night's Socceroos' goals. "Y'know, I actually pulled off most of those moves myself last season. I was slotting goals from all angles."

"Really? I thought the Bullfrogs only scored three goals for the whole year." I said, confused. "Maybe I heard wrong. I'll check with Dash."

Jules went red, "Oh, I wouldn't bother. We should probably focus on the future instead."

"Totally." I said, patting my sports bag that held the precious Socceroos jumper. "And thanks to this little beauty I'm going to be a part of it."

I couldn't stop myself powerwalking to get to there. Pity Jules had to keep correcting my route. "No, dude. LEFT!"

We ran into Dash and Izzy at the gate. "Morning Soccerufus!" said Dash. And for the briefest second I thought I noticed Izzy smile too. But maybe she was just mid hiccup or something.

Down by the bay, the soccer pitch looked MAGICAL.

The grass had that freshly mowed smell and was covered with morning dew. I couldn't help admiring the striped pattern on the field.

Everything was in readiness for the game. Gleaming white nets had been attached to the goals, the yellow corner flags flapped in the breeze and Coach Wentworth was putting in place the last few balloons and streamers to decorate the clubrooms in Bullfrogs colours.

A few of my soon-to-be teammates were already warming up; Tom and Pete were passing to each other, Olivia was heading balls to Clara, and Happy Hughes was doing some stretches with a typically glum look on his face.

Some members of our opposition—the Fernside

Falcons—were talking tactics up the other end.

The stage was set. And I had my heart set on a STARRING ROLE.

We crossed the pitch to the clubrooms. The simple *piff* sound the ball made as kids passed it among themselves was suddenly one of the most exciting noises I'd ever heard. And that includes the school bell on a Friday arvo.

Coach Wentworth had disappeared inside the clubrooms. I paused for a moment, wondering whether I should follow him in or wait until he came out. He and I needed to have a very important conversation. And I had to get it right.

"Whoa, you okay Rufus? Looks like you're constipated!" said Jules.

"Jules!" said Dash.

"Sorry," I said. "Guess that's my thinking face. I have to chat with the coach."

"If you want my advice," smiled Dash. "Stop thinking and just go and talk to him. Show Coach Wentworth the jersey and all will be forgiven. For sure!"

"Want me to butter him up, dude?" asked Jules. "He *loves* me!"

"No!" cried Dash, "Sorry Jules. I mean, let Soccerufus sort this one out for himself."

I started walking into the clubrooms, only to pass by the Turner Twins.

"Wow! Soccerufus! We didn't expect to see *you* here."

"You rejected old Wentworth remember? Said you didn't want to be a Bullfrog."

"Yep. I remember." I said. "My memory's pretty good actually. I'll *never* forget that you guys tried to steal my prize yesterday."

"Steal?"

"Lighten up, *dufus*. Can't take a joke?"

They both smiled big evil grins. I wasn't sure I'd ever find those two funny.

I started to shake a little as I entered the rooms.

The main room inside had a canteen at one end. This was where Coach Wentworth had plastered all his soccer memorabilia. Weirdly, everything smelt like mothballs and old hotdog water.

Coach Wentworth had his back to me. He was straightening a framed pair of boots that belonged to someone called Thierry Henry. Or did I read that backwards? Surely it was meant to be Henry...?

Coach Wentworth spun around. Tall and thin, leering over me with his eyes magnified by his glasses. It felt like they were STARING INTO MY SOUL.

"Rudy," he said. "What are you doing here?"

"It's Rufus, coach."

"For a young man who doesn't want to be on the soccer team you're sure taking a keen interest in the sport. I trust you enjoyed the game last night?"

"Um, yes. I did. Um. Look, well…" I took the Socceroos jumper out of my bag hoping it would help me stop blabbering. "Coach Wentworth, I… Um."

"Spit it out, son. I have the Bullfrogs game to prepare for." He straightened his tie and flicked a few specks of dust from his jacket.

"Well, I just wanted to say sorry for ruining one of your signed caps yesterday."

"Is that so?" said the coach.

"And to make up for it, I wanted to give you this." I handed him the Socceroos jumper.

Coach Wentworth's eyes LIT UP. He suddenly reminded me of Principal Humpton visiting the pancake stall during the recent school fair. They had set it up on the soccer pitch. Pity no one remembered the sprinklers were on a timer. Bit of a downer when they went off.

"So, um, Coach Wentworth, I... *Coach Wentworth?*" I said.

Coach Wentworth was a million miles away, staring at the jumper, tracing the signatures with his index finger.

"Coach?"

"Hmm?"

"There's one other thing." I said. "I was hoping you might let me become a Bullfrog after all."

"You want to be what?" said Coach Wentworth, his big eyes locking onto me once more.

"I'd like to join the school soccer team." I said. "Please."

Coach Wentworth cleared his throat. Something

about his face softened. "Firstly, thank you kindly for the jumper. Your apology is accepted."

He was saying what I wanted to hear but something didn't seem right.

"The thing is, son, in terms of playing for the Bullfrogs, registrations closed on the last working day of the month."

"The what did what?" I said. At least I think I said something like that, it was difficult to tell given the way my stomach was swirling.

"I'm sorry, young Rufus, but your paperwork needed to be submitted to the League yesterday. We're low on numbers as it is, so having you on the team would've been a big help. But February is as good as gone, son. Jolly awful timing."

I was confused. My mind raced. "What are you saying?"

"Rufus, it's too late. I'm afraid you can't join the team."

10

THE INCIDENT

left the clubrooms in a daze.

Jules immediately came up to me to and tried to give me a high five. "Welcome to the Bullfrogs, dude! Another teammate lucky enough to say they shared the pitch with the great Jules!"

I just kept walking. Not out to the pitch. I turned left.

I think I was heading for the lake. I had a vague desire to start skimming stones and pretend I was back by the creek on the farm. Back where I belonged.

Dash got in my way. "What happened?"

"Dude, you look sadder than Happy Hughes." said Jules.

I didn't know what to say. I thought I'd finally found

my thing here at Bayview. Not only did I enjoy soccer but I knew it made my parents pleased to think I was settling in. WIN-WIN. But no. All of a sudden, it was big time LOSE-LOSE.

"You gave him the jumper, r-r-right?" Dash asked.

I nodded.

"Well, that should've totally got you in his good books." said Jules. "What went wrong?"

I didn't feel like talking. But Jules and Dash wanted answers. Fortunately, Izzy stood in their way and made room to let me keep on walking. It was her way of telling them to leave me alone.

Then, from the corner of my eye, I saw it. Beside the clubrooms. The VERY LAST THING I wanted to see at that moment. The most EVIL OBJECT in the UNIVERSE. It was right there, sitting in the grass, trying to look innocent.

A cricket ball.

"What are *you* looking at?" I yelled at the ball. "LEAVE ME ALONE!"

That was enough to draw Dash, Jules and Izzy back to me.

"W-w-what's going on?" asked Dash, wide eyed.

"You cool?" said Jules.

Izzy tensed up, glancing around for some kind of threat.

"It's just *that* thing." I pointed at the ball.

I noticed Jules shoot Dash a confused look. "Dude, you feeling okay?"

"You know that's just a cricket ball, right?" asked Dash with a gentle *has-he-lost-it?* smile.

"Of course I know it's a cricket ball!" I snapped.

Dash took half a step back.

"Sorry." I said. I let out a huge sigh, then slumped up against the side of the clubrooms. "It's just that that little thing reminded me of the *INCIDENT*."

"The what?"

"The INCIDENT." I said. "That's what I call it. The whole reason Mum and Dad moved from Biggins Valley to Bayview in the first place. It was all my fault."

"I don't follow, dude?"

Out on the field, most of the Bullfrogs had arrived by now. Coach Wentworth was starting to gather the team together for some warm-up drills.

"You need to go." I said, nodding towards the pitch.

"That can wait." said Dash. "What were you saying?"

I shrugged. What did it matter? I couldn't go back in time and change anything anyway. Even in my dreams I stuff that up too.

"You were saying that *you* were the whole reason your family had to move here to Bayview," said Jules. "You did some major stuff up or something. Sounds super full on terrible."

"*Thanks* Jules." said Dash. "I'm sure it wasn't quite that b-b-bad."

"Actually it kind of was." I said. "Guess I might as well tell you now."

Dash, Jules and Izzy perched on the grass beside me. I felt flat. I felt stupid. And I felt like spewing up my banana breakfast. But despite it all, it was nice to have my new friends by my side.

"I don't really like talking about the INCIDENT but I guess it was bound to come up sooner or later." I said.

"When did it happen dude, sometime last year?" asked Jules.

"Yep. Just before Christmas. I was still at my old school. It was all because I missed the bus. See, the ride home used to take over an hour. That meant there wasn't much time for hobbies—y'know, sports and stuff. But on that particular day, because I'd missed the bus, my mate Callum convinced me to tag along with him to cricket practice while I waited for my mum to come and pick me up."

"But you weren't a cricketer?" asked Dash, trying to piece it all together.

"Not for a second. I'd barely even picked up a cricket bat before. But when it was my turn to bat I remember Callum saying to me, 'See if you can score a run. For a guy like you, that'll be like scoring a century.'"

"What did he m-m-mean by that?" said Dash.

"No idea." I said. "But anyway as one of my school mates bowled the cricket ball at me a crow nearby squawked.

REAL loud. So I flinched, and I accidently swung the bat. It connected with the ball and I hit a massive shot."

Jules put two hands up in the air, "Six!"

"Six what?"

"Don't worry, dude. Carry on."

"Anyway, the ball soared through the air. Suddenly I was super pumped that I'd managed to make such a shot. But the feeling didn't last long because just at that moment our school Principal was driving out of the school car park in his new sports car."

"Uh oh." said Jules, miming a bomb dropping.

"Yep. That's right. The ball dipped down through the air—the timing couldn't have been better if I'd tried—and it smashed into the front windscreen of the principal's car."

"Ah, so that's how the cricket ball fits in." said Dash, tapping the ball beside her. "Super glad you weren't just yelling at random sports gear."

"But the INCIDENT didn't end there. My old school was way different from Bayview. We were surrounded by paddocks. Well, when the principal's car was hit by the ball he swerved and crashed through the fence of a paddock. And guess what was in that paddock: a BULL."

"Oh." said Dash.

"Totally. The bull took off."

"Double oh." said Jules.

"The bull was wild. He ploughed straight through the flower bed that was shaped to look like our school logo. And then knocked over the statue of our region's founder, the honourable Reginald Biggins."

"Sorry Reggie." said Jules. "But I guess it could've been worse."

"It was. The bull was now going nuts, and started heading for us out on the oval. He knocked over a goal post that crashed and missed Callum by millimetres. Then it started coming for me."

"I hope you h-h-held onto your cricket bat for protection."

"I did. But luckily I didn't need it. I'm not sure whether it was the car's spluttering engine or just its shiny red paint job, but the bull suddenly turned around and charged at the car. The Principal was still behind the wheel trying to get the car untangled from the fence."

"Not g-g-good." said Dash.

"No, not good at all." I said. "The cricketers had raced off in all directions but I could only stand there and stare as the bull rocketed towards the sports car. Just as it was about to collide, the principal got the car moving. But he could only get it to skid back half a metre. Which meant the huge beast tried to change course at the last second and..."

Dash and Jules leant in closer. Izzy remained still.

"And w-w-what?" said Dash.

"The bull stumbled as it leapt at the car—like a bullfrog, not a bull—and landed IN THE BACK SEAT!"

"Whoa."

"And I believe, in the panic soon after, the bull may have used the back seat as a toilet."

"Eww. Nasty."

"Obviously, the principal wasn't happy. He isn't quite as jolly as our Humpty. In fact I never saw my old principal laugh. But after the INCIDENT. I definitely saw him cry. His flashy new car was a wreck."

No one said anything for a few seconds. I wondered what they were thinking. I caught Jules' eye.

"Well, that's quite an incident, all right." said Jules. "Yep, very much an incident."

"Okay Bullfrogs, the moment's arrived. Bring it in!" called Coach Wentworth, officially starting the warm-up. Dash, Jules and Izzy got to their feet. Dash didn't seem to know what to say. So she just gave me a smile.

I looked over at the team. And then my morning actually got worse. I spotted Mum up on the hill, walking down from the school. She'd been so excited about me getting into the soccer team that she must have come to watch me play.

My throat suddenly went dry.

Mum was about to be MAJORLY disappointed.

II

A LEAP OF FAITH

"**M**um, hello there." I said, trying to sound normal. "What a delight to see you here."

"A *delight*?" She said. "What's wrong?"

I'd run over to intercept her on the boundary closest to the school. But breaking the bad news gently wasn't going exactly according to plan. Possibly because I didn't have a plan.

"Nothing's wrong." I laughed nervously.

"Good. I thought I'd come to watch you play your first ever soccer match."

"Right. Well, about that…"

"What's up, mister? Is everything okay?"

I couldn't answer. I just dropped my head.

"Rufus?"

"They won't let me on the team, Mum."

"Oh, Rufus." she said, giving me a big squishy hug. "Really? How come?"

"I'm not sure." I said, quickly breaking out of the hug. I may have been upset but I was still aware that we were in plain view of all my new schoolmates. "Something about late paperwork. Something about registration. Missing the League's cut off date or something."

"Is that so." said Mum, pulling her iPad from her bag. She started tapping away.

That didn't really impress me. I wished she wasn't so obsessed with her new job as a hotshot lawyer. Here I was having a major crisis and she'd decided it was the perfect time to check her emails.

"I'll just go get my gear and maybe we can head off?" I said, remembering I'd left my bag in the clubrooms.

Mum didn't respond. Too busy. Probably trying to find the right emoji for workaholic. So I just started crossing the field. I was GUTTED. I hadn't felt this bad since Mum and Dad announced that we had to move.

The Bullfrogs were huddled around Coach Wentworth.
I tried not to look at them as I passed by.

PIFFF!

A ball hit me on the back of my head.
I looked over at the team. The Turner Twins were
laughing. Dash was giving them a filthy look.

"Now, listen up, Bullfrogs, and you'd best listen
closely." demanded Coach Wentworth. "Pretend I'm
Ange Postecoglou, the Socceroos coach himself."

Had the Turner Twins kicked the ball at me on

purpose? Probably. Then I saw Tim Turner stretch out his leg to try and smack another ball in my direction.

"Yeeeoooh!" He yelled as he kicked the ball.

He grabbed his leg.

"Uh, oh." said Todd Turner.

"What's happened, son?" asked Coach Wentworth.

"I think I've pulled a muscle." said Tim Turner.

"Really?" asked Coach Wentworth, flustered. "Well, did you do a warm-up?"

Tim Turner shook his head. He was gritting his teeth. I could almost feel the PAIN myself. I found the medical kit among the equipment on the sidelines and ran it over.

"Um, thanks Rufus." said Todd Turner.

Coach Wentworth checked out Tim Turner's leg. "I'm sorry to say, young Timothy, that it appears you've strained your hamstring."

"Done a hammy?" said Jules. "Dude, that sucks."

Coach Wentworth took an instant ice pack from the medical kit and squeezed it. "Hold this against your muscle."

By then Mr Turner had run over. I assumed he was the twins' dad because he looked exactly like them but with a goatee. Mr Turner, Coach Wentworth and Izzy helped Tim Turner to the sidelines.

Then the vampire, I mean umpire, I mean *referee* blew her whistle. Despite the dramatic injury, it was time to start the game.

"But we're a man down!" said Isaac—and when it came to numbers he was proving ever reliable. "What are we going to do?"

"I'm afraid there's only one thing we can do." said Coach Wentworth as he stormed back over to the group.

"Ask the Falcons to postpone the game?" suggested Dash.

"Or just let *me* carry the team, as usual." said Jules.

"Nope. We have to take one of the Falcons out." suggested Karate Kevin (the tall one). Then the other Kevin mimed a karate chop.

"No, no, no. None of that." said Coach Wentworth. "We need to offer to forfeit the game. We don't have enough players. The Falcons will take the points."

"Not so fast." called Mum as she ran over to us, iPad in hand.

"Who on earth are you?" asked Coach Wentworth, who wasn't coping well with all the fuss.

"Why, I am Rufus' mother." said Mum, as if she was claiming to be the Queen or something. "*And* I'm also a lawyer. You need to let my son join the Bullfrogs, right now."

I grabbed Mum by the hand, dragging her away from the group before she embarrassed me any further. The way she was going it was a miracle she hadn't called out, "OBJECTION!"

Coach Wentworth huffed and puffed as he followed us. "Look, I'm dreadfully sorry, Mrs *Rufus*. But your son has missed the registration cut off date. Simple as that."

"The last workday of the month, correct?" said Mum reading from her iPad. "That's what it says here on the League's website."

Had my mum been googling that whole time? Suddenly I felt bad for doubting her.

"Yes, that's correct." said Coach Wentworth. "And the last workday day of the month was yesterday, Friday 26th of February."

"Actually this is a leap year," said Mum.

"Beg yours?" said Coach Wentworth.

"Which means you can submit the paperwork this Monday, the 29th February. Therefore, Rufus can play!"

"What?" I said.

Coach Wentworth got his phone out and checked the calendar. "Leap year. So it is. Heavens. Well that settles it."

"Does this mean…" I mumbled.

"You bet it does!" said Mum triumphantly.

Coach Wentworth shook my hand, "You're a Bullfrog, Rufus!"

And although it didn't sound quite as magical as the famous line, "You're a wizard, Harry." I was THRILLED to hear it, none-the-less.

"Awesome!" said Dash who was not-so-subtly eavesdropping.

Mum spoke with the referee, and convinced the ref to start the game ten minutes late, which gave me time to run to the rooms and get changed. Coach Wentworth gave me the number 10 jumper. I was happy with that. I now knew it was Archie Thompson's number and it also happened to be the amount of party pies I can eat in one sitting. (Without spewing that is. With spewing, it's a whole other story.)

The crowd had built up as I'd received my jumper. Parents and schoolmates lined both sides of the pitch. I couldn't really tell who was barracking for who, the only thing I knew for sure was there were way more people watching than I would've liked. This was my first match after all.

Coach Wentworth called us in for a final huddle.

He used those big eyes of his to glare at each one of us. "Bullfrogs. This is it. A new season. A chance to start again. We've had a jolly good pre-season, we've even had a pep talk from Archie Thompson no less, and we've had the Socceroos giving us coaching tips. Plus we have a new recruit, young Rufus."

Coach Wentworth gestured towards me.

"That would be *Soccerufus*, coach," said Dash.

I edged behind Izzy. It was nice to be mentioned, but I wasn't sure I was going to make much difference.

"As most of you are probably aware, the Falcons are a new team. So perhaps this will give us the chance to get the jump on them before they start to learn to play as a team."

"Yeah!" cried Pete.

"Come on, let's do it!" yelled Llama.

"We definitely don't want to start the year with another loss!" said Todd Turner, who'd already forgotten about his brother's injury.

I expected Coach Wentworth to reply by saying something like 'winning isn't everything' and that it was all about 'how you play the game' or some of the other lessons you're supposed to learn from soppy Hollywood movies. But he just sighed and simply said, "Indeed." Perhaps all those losses had got to him.

The Falcons were pumping each other up with 'woohoos' and 'come ons'. They looked slick and cool and pretty much COMPLETELY UNLIKE US. They gave off a vibe like they were proud horses, while we seemed more like dazed donkeys.

"Eyes on me." said Coach Wentworth. "Mark my words, Bullfrogs, we're in with a jolly good shot today. So you get out there and give it all you've got!"

All my teammates started riddupping—which drew a few looks from the Falcons' supporters—but I couldn't bring myself to do it. I hadn't earned it yet.

Then we burst out onto the pitch.

This was a little awkward for me because according to Jules I was pretty much already in position, so I only needed to take two steps. Coach Wentworth had me playing right back. I immediately worked out who was playing left back, and pretty much planned to copy absolutely everything he did, just on my side of the field. It was Stinkin' Lincoln. He was picking a wedgie. Okay. Maybe I wouldn't do ABSOLUTELY everything.

I was tingling with goose bumps all over. I wasn't sure if that was because it was a cold morning or because I was more nervous than a long-tailed cat in a room full of rocking chairs (as my Dad would say). Probably both.

My opponent was a stocky dude with dreadlocks who had a monobrow you'd need hedge cutters to tame and legs that were thicker than my waist. He offered me his hand. As we shook I felt like every bone in my hand was about to shatter.

"Nice to meet you." I blurted out without thinking.

"Funny." He replied. Though I was pretty sure he didn't really think so.

I glanced around the ground. We were all in position. THIS WAS REALLY HAPPENING! Dreadlocks was jogging on the spot. Onlookers probably thought I was doing the same but in reality I was so anxious I couldn't keep still.

The ref blew her whistle.

This took me by surprise. I nearly choked on my mouth guard. Clara—also in defence—ran over and whacked me on the back. I spat out the mouthguard.

"Thanks." I coughed.

Dreadlocks looked at me like I was some kind of alien. And not an impressive one, I might add. The ref was watching me too, making sure the moment had passed. I gave her a thumbs up, whacking the mouthguard back in place.

I was thrilled that Mum's super-lawyer skills had

helped me get a place on the team. But was I kidding myself? Would the Bullfrogs be better off with me playing?

And was I just setting myself up to somehow cause another INCIDENT?

Guess I was about to find out.

Dash took the kick off. And she passed the ball to me.

12

FIRST HALF FREAK OUT

My legs were spaghetti.

The ball was rolling straight to me.

There was a blur of movement all around. Players were closing in.

Someone was screaming. AUUUUUUUGH!

Then I realised that someone was me. I was FREAKING OUT BIG TIME!

The ball hit my feet. Suddenly I was surrounded. My teammates were all calling for the pass. The Falcons were right on me. I was angling my feet this way and that. Should I pass left? Should I pass right?

Then I tripped over the ball.

"Oooof." I face-planted.

Rumbling feet passed me by. I got myself upright.
The Falcons had taken possession. They were streaming
towards goal. I had to drop back and help.

The Falcons passed easily to one other. Once, twice,
three times, with pinpoint accuracy. They may have
been a new team but the way they combined looked like
they'd been playing together for years.

A curly-haired girl had the ball at the corner of the
box. I spotted a tall redhead boy from the Falcons, all
alone in the centre. I remembered our practice match
outside the stadium the night before: the long pass from
Curls to Big Red was on for sure.

PIFFF!

The ball sailed by Stinkin' Lincoln and Clara, straight
to Redhead. I CHARGED at him trying to muster up the
aggression of that troublesome bull from my old school.
I'm not sure if it was because Redhead heard me coming or
not, but he fumbled and wasn't able to trap the ball cleanly.
It spilt just ahead of him. And that's when Izzy swooped.

She was even FIERCER than a bull. She thundered out
of the penalty box from the goals and hoofed the ball
high and far away. (I think NASA might still be looking
for it on its way to the moon, honestly.)

Phew. Izzy had saved us. But Dash was the only one
who acknowledged it. She gave Izzy a fist pump.

"Nice work, Izzy!" I yelled. Seemed the least
I could do.

Izzy returned to the goals and simply pointed up field.

Todd Turner and Llama were passing to each other.
They'd crossed the half way line. Woo-hoo!

The other Bullfrogs started pushing forward, so
I did the same, all the while puffing like crazy. I hadn't
run this hard since the time I thought I'd spotted a wild

panther back on our farm. It turned out it was actually a burnt log, but you can never be too careful.

The Falcons had numbers deep in their defensive half, so we had to pass the ball around, holding possession, while looking for an opportunity to get close enough for a shot. (At least that's what I thought was happening, I wasn't really 100% across the tactics.)

The ball went back and forth between Izzy and Dash and Jules and Todd Turner and Isaac, just past the centreline. But then Isaac miskicked to Tom and the Falcons intercepted and sped into attack.

A short speedy Falcon quickly got herself within range and took a shot.

Off target. LUCKY.

Izzy kicked the ball out. We worked the ball again through the centre but again the Falcons won it back. They pushed forward and had another shot at goal.

This time it was right on target, but Izzy dived. Her legs seemed spring-loaded. She made a great save.

Izzy was working overtime. We were under the pump. Sooner or later one of the Falcons' shots was going to find the back of the net. Our game plan, if we had one, was failing. I wasn't entirely certain what our plan was. But I could tell it wasn't doing what it was meant to.

"We're getting smashed." said Todd Turner, gasping for breath.

"But at least they're not scoring." I said, puffing hard while trying to look on the bright side. But then I probably wasn't the best person to analyse the game.

"Rufus is right." said Dash. "But it's time we put some pressure on *their* goalie and stepped up *our* attack."

"Yeah. Let's do a step-attack! Woo!" I cried, pretty sure I wasn't quite nailing the lingo.

"We can do this, Bullfrogs!" yelled Llama. It was nice to hear her being optimistic. Maybe she'd learned something from the night before.

"Totally!" cried Jules. "Just wait till *I* turn it on."

"We've been waiting since your first game." muttered Happy Hughes.

"Oi!" said Jules.

Izzy rolled the ball out of the box to Clara who started a very impressive dribble from deep in defence. Clara screwed her nose up when she was angry and right at that moment I'd never seen another nose quite like it. She worked her way past Redhead and shot the ball inside to Llama. With defenders approaching, Llama flicked the ball back to me.

Spaghetti legs again!

I tried to trap the ball but only succeeded in knocking it sideways. Fortunately it went to Olivia, running free.

Olivia dribbled through the centre. She ZOOMED by two Falcons, pumping her arms like an Olympic sprinter. Then she passed the ball straight between a Falcon's legs to Dash.

"Nutmeg!" cried Jules.

I had to admit it seemed a little strange to be requesting an exotic spice at a time like that.

Dash pretended to go one way, then back-heeled the ball around a Falcon defender. She SCOOPED the ball up with her foot, floating it high to Frankie in the centre. He headed the ball and DRILLED it towards goal.

The Falcon goalie leaped. The ball was out of his reach. This was it!

BOOOOOING!

The ball bounced off the crossbar.

No goal.

"Oooooh!" cried the crowd.

On the sidelines, Coach Wentworth slammed his fist on his clipboard. Alongside him, on the bench, Tim Turner shook his head. It was the most he could do given his leg was elevated. Further along, Principal Humpty just shrugged. I spotted Mum too. She was clapping.

"Good effort, Bullfrogs." cried Mum. "Keep it up!" Always positive is Mum.

The Falcon keeper booted the ball long and high, and it was headed straight for me. Nearby, a Falcon with a fiercely tight ponytail was zeroing in on both me and the ball. Her hairstyle was so slicked back I could only assume it was done up to help her pace. If anything my own 'do probably held me back but that's the price you pay for style. I'd just have to sprint extra hard to beat her. And I did. But the ball bounced. RIGHT OVER MY HEAD.

I dropped further back into defence—almost tripping myself up—desperate to beat Ponytail to the ball.

But this time, I overran the ball, and it settled at her feet. How far had we run? Was she close enough to take a shot? How the heck was I going to stop her? I turned around and faced her, just metres away.

THUMP!

Ponytail kicked low and hard.

Then I stuffed up.

I don't know why, but I dived and put my hand out. I stopped the ball. It smacked into the palm of my hand.

"Yeeouch." It stung. But I forgot about that almost straight away. My stomach dropped. And not because I'd overdone it with the bananas. I began tingling all over. One word ran through my head: Stupid, stupid, STUPID!

Weeeeeeeht! The ref blew her whistle. "Hand ball. Free kick to the Falcons."

I doubled over, panting. Todd Turner came up beside me. "I know you're new to the game but there is *one* basic rule you should have worked out by now."

There was NOTHING I could say. Todd Turner was right. I was reeling. I could feel everyone's eyes on me. It was making me woozy. And my face had gone red hot. I didn't dare look to the bench. I could only imagine how much Coach Wentworth's glasses had fogged up.

Fortunately, I'd given away a free just *outside* the penalty box. But Ponytail was well within range. She positioned herself for her run up and was getting set to take a shot.

13

GOOOOOOAL!

"**B**uild a wall!" yelled Dash, then she looked at me. "Tell 'em Rufus!"

More than ever, I didn't really feel like anyone should be taking instructions from me, especially after my handball. But Dash nudged me. Hard.

"Yeah," I yelled, waving my arms like a windmill, "start building. It's wall time! Wall. Wall... WALL!"

What on Earth was I talking about?

But Pete, Isaac, Todd Turner and Happy Hughes rushed over to join. We seemed to be standing in a line of five, facing Ponytail who was about to kick. Now I remembered. I'd seen the Manchester United guys building a wall on TV last night.

Then everyone started grabbing their... Um... Well. Everyone had their hands in front of their, um... Let's just say they all PROTECTED themselves. It seemed foolish to leave myself exposed too, so I covered myself with my hands as well. Was this normal? I snuck a peek over at Mum but she and the others didn't seem to be making anything of it. Perhaps this was a team bonding thing or something?

Ponytail ran in and...
THWAAACK!

She booted the ball.

I closed my eyes. I had no idea where the ball actually went, but I did hear a massive WOOOOOSSSH. But when I opened my eyes again, Izzy had the ball safely in her hands. She took a few steps and HOOFED it all the way into our forward line.

"Splendid save, Isabella!" cried Coach Wentworth from the sidelines, his glasses now well and truly unfogged again.

I wasn't used to this much excitement. Back on the farm we considered it a big day if one of the cows got loose.

Before I even had a chance to breath, the Falcons stole the ball back. Redhead passed to Dreadlocks. As he THUNDERED into our half I was certain I could feel minor tremors rumble across the pitch. The closer he got the weaker I felt. He had the ball at his feet and it wasn't about to disobey him.

"He's *your* man, Rufus!" yelled Llama.

"You can have him." I muttered. "I'm not picky."

Dreadlocks was now just a few metres away. There was nowhere to hide. Believe me, I checked.

"Block him, Rufus!" cried Pete.

Block him? Sure. But how, exactly?

"You've got to do something, superstar!" yelled Todd Turner. "Anything!"

My mind reeled. For a split second I wondered if I could distract him with a version of *Gangnam Style* or was that too 2012? But Gangnam wasn't far off what I was doing. I wiggled one way then wiggled back. Then he was RIGHT ON ME.

"That's it. Sheep-dog him!" cried Dash.

Sheepdog? I thought of old Bluey. He would do whatever it took to get in the way of any dumb sheep who was trying to escape the pack. Bluey would've known what to do with the dreaded Dreadlocks. He'd have held him up. Taken his space. Given him no option.

I sidestepped in front of Dreadlocks. He balked towards the centre and flicked the ball out to the wing. But I was sheep-dogging. I wasn't sucked in by his manoeuvre because I had kept my eyes on his hips. I moved out wide with him.

We went toe-to-toe along the wing. He had all the tricky footwork but I stayed in his way and forced him to run diagonally towards the far edge of the pitch.

The only problem was that we'd dropped deep into our defence. The goals had to be getting close.

"Keep goalside, dude!" yelled Jules.

Then I noticed Dreadlocks narrow his eyes. He was lining up for a shot. With everything I had I THREW my foot at the ball.

SMACKKK!

He booted the ball. But it brushed my leg. It was knocked off course and sailed wide of the goals. Yeah!

"Nice one, Rufus!" Mum called from the sidelines. Maybe I was starting to get the hang of this game after all.

"Corner!" cried the ref.

It took me a moment to work out what the ref meant.

"Drop back, Rufus. The Falcons have got a corner kick," yelled Llama as she streamed past me. "We need everyone back to defend the goals."

She was right. Apart from Dash, the other Bullfrogs were taking their time.

"Help out, Bullfrogs!" I yelled. "Come on!"

"You heard him." yelled Dash. "Get down here and get amongst it!"

It was nice to hear Dash in full voice. And stutter free—again. "Hey Dash, thanks for the tip about *sheep-dogging.*"

"No worries, that's just what my Dad calls it, but I thought it might make sense to you too." Dash said.

GOOOOOOAL!

Dreadlocks placed the ball carefully in the corner, under the flag and took a few steps back. By now, plenty of players—ours and theirs—had dropped into the penalty box. Izzy was screaming, "Give me space!" The Falcons were moving around like they had ANTS IN THEIR PANTS. Hah! If only.

"Get on the front post, Clara." shouted Olivia, as she hovered around the far post, leaving the goal mouth to Izzy. "Seriously, I shouldn't have to tell you this."

"First game back.' I said. "We're probably all a little crusty."

"Think you mean rusty?" whispered Dash.

"Not in Stinkin' Lincoln's case.' said Jules, as Lincoln picked something out of his hair and ate it.

Dreadlocks was ready. He took a few steps towards the ball. I heard Izzy grunting and glanced over to see her eyes were glued on the ball. She may have technically been a BullFROG, but the face she wore actually made her look more like a bullDOG.

THWUUUMP!

Dreadlocks booted the ball.

It soared high, while curving our way. Everyone was jostling around me. I struggled to stay upright, caught in the middle of the pack as the ball flew at us. Some players

jumped, others dived, but the ball was just too high for us. And it was on track to go straight into the net.

WHHHOOOOOMP!

Izzy had BURST through the pack and punched the ball into orbit. It's pretty surprising the ball didn't explode on impact. She'd crashed through a pack of Falcons and Bulldogs all now slowly picking themselves up from the turf.

I scrambled to my feet. A Falcon booted the ball back towards us. I found myself closest to it, and took the ball at my feet, as most of the other Bullfrogs were still getting upright.

Uh-oh. The Falcon striker was coming at me. Fast. I panicked. I passed back to Izzy. Surely that was the safe bet. It was easy to see why Jules reckoned Izzy was destined for a career as impressive as the former Aussie goalie Mark Schwarzer.

Only problem was I kicked the ball WAY TOO HARD.

"No, no, no, no, no, NOOOOO!"

Izzy was wrong-footed. The ball whizzed past her and straight into the net. She stared at me with big wild eyes. I dropped my head.

The Falcons cheered and hugged each other.

"You just scored an *own goal*!" said Todd Turner.

"Some star new recruit you are! You've put the Falcons in front. We're one nil down."

I collapsed onto the ground. This was EXACTLY the sort of thing I'd been afraid of.

DISASTER. Another INCIDENT.

14

SUCKERUFUS

The name's Rufus. SUCKERufus.

I felt like a total sucker for letting myself get involved in this soccer thing in the first place. Why did I put myself out there? Again?

I should've learnt my lesson from the INCIDENT.

I'm a catastrophe magnet. That's me. How could I have been so stupid?

Thanks to my 'own goal', suddenly the Bullfrogs were right under the pump. The ball mostly stayed in our defence until half-time. To be honest, I tried to avoid it. No one seemed that keen to pass it to me, anyway.

Izzy saved three more big shots on goal. She had the ball in her hands again when the whistle blew for the break. I trudged after the others as they left the field. We were all dragging our feet as we filed into the clubrooms.

"Don't stress, Rufus." said Dash. "You've made a huge difference, trust me."

I said nothing. She may have thought so but I certainly didn't.

I slumped against the wall, towards the back of the group. I gulped on my water bottle, but squeezed it too hard and water squirted all over me.

GIMME A BREAK!

Yep, catastrophe magnet, that's me.

Orange segments were passed around. Everyone munched in silence. Even Jules was quiet. MIRACLE. The other Bullfrogs seemed deflated. I guess they were hoping this season might be different to the last. That a victory might be just around the corner. Right now we couldn't even see the corner. In fact we were facing a big WRONG WAY GO BACK sign.

Principal Humpton entered, oddly upbeat. But that may have been due to the oranges he grabbed from the pile. "Mmm, juicy.'

My brain started ticking over. Had I really just lost the game for us? I didn't want to believe it. I thought to myself what Mum had said: that I'd be great for the team. She reckoned I'd be POSITIVE, that I'd WORK HARD and that most of all I'd NEVER GIVE UP.

"What was that?" asked Happy Hughes, to my left. "Did you really just mutter *never give up*?"

"Good advice from Rufus. We're only one goal down." said Isaac, our numbers man. "Come on guys, we're not out of it."

I agreed. "We're still in with a chance aren't we? One goal is nothing."

Plus, I thought to myself, the Falcons didn't even score that goal. I DID.

"Maybe if they weren't twice as fast as us." complained Frankie.

"Is there a way round that?" I asked, as my brain whirred. "A clever tic-tac?"

"You mean, a *tactic*?" said Llama.

I laughed at my slip of the tongue. She laughed too. So did Dash, Pete and Tom.

"I guess we could try lots of quick passes." said Llama, putting her captain's brain in gear. "We can't outrun the Falcons but maybe we can move the ball fast enough to keep it off them."

Todd Turner piped up, "Okay Rufus, this is great and all, but if you're so smart, how do we stop them getting so many shots on goal?"

Izzy grunted, she barely ever said a word but we all knew she must've been getting worn out. She'd been copping it big time.

"Well, I'm no expert." I said.

"You can say that again," muttered Todd Turner.

"But, if the Falcons keep speeding through the gaps in our defence, let's plug the gaps."

"A zone defence?" said Llama. "Brilliant. Man-on-man isn't working, it's time to switch it up. Good one, Rufus."

"Might ease the pressure on Izzy." I said. "She's been taking a pounding out there.'

Everyone agreed. I started clapping her, but it seemed that wasn't really the thing to do in these situations. "Um. Carry on."

"Zone defence. That's fine, but that won't help us score." said Todd Turner.

"Well that's simple." I said. "We need to get the ball to Dash, in space. She's our gun striker, right?"

Dash went bright red. But from what I'd heard it was true. Whether the Turner Twins liked it or not.

"She's our best chance, wouldn't you say, Todd?" I asked.

Everyone looked at Todd Turner. He said nothing for a second. This simple question seemed to be just as painful to him as straining a hammy had been to his brother, Tim. He glanced at Dash. "Yep. Agreed."

Dash smiled. I was tempted to start clapping again but I'd learnt my lesson.

Jules cleared his throat, "I'm *also* a bit of a gun." Silence.

"Goes without saying, I guess." added Jules.

I sucked on another orange. I could see the team was thinking over the new tactics. But they didn't seem one hundred percent sold yet. Truth is, I really had no clue if any of it would work, I was just blurting out ideas that I'd heard mainly from watching the soccer on TV with Mum the night before.

I stuffed my drink bottle in my bag and heard a crunch. There was a piece of paper inside. A drawing. Clearly done by my sister, Rikki.

I smiled at the thought that this was how Rikki saw me; as a soccerstar! Suddenly I was more determined than ever to play my guts out. We hadn't lost yet. There was another half of football to go!

"Right then, Bullfrogs." said Coach Wentworth— sounding like a drill sergeant—as he entered the room holding a blank wooden picture frame. "Once again we have a challenge on our hands." He was staring straight at me.

I shrunk into myself, trying to disappear into the wall behind me.

"But before you get back out on the field, I want you all to take a good, hard look at this empty frame."

A couple of Bullfrogs exchanged glances. Stinkin' Lincoln peered at the frame as if it was some sort of optical illusion.

"Feast your eyes, Bullfrogs." said Coach Wentworth.

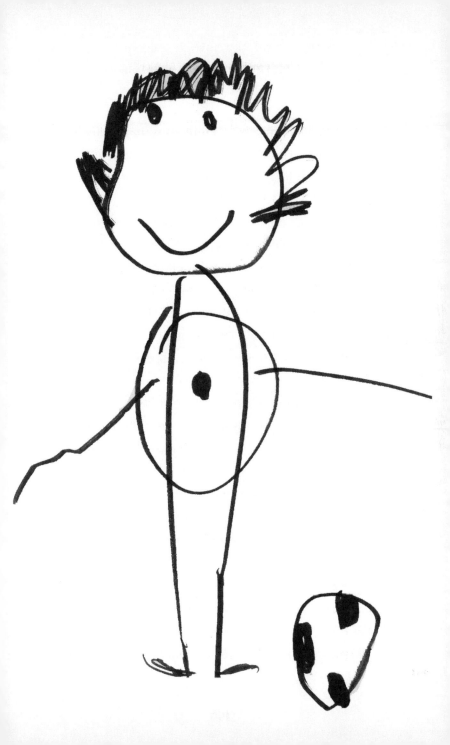

Humpty leaned in to take a look as well. He chuckled. "Coach Wentworth, I'm afraid the frame's empty."

"Exactly." said Coach Wentworth, glaring at us all. "But not for long."

"Is he working on a magic act?" I whispered to Jules.

"Dude. If he is, it's not a very good one."

"Bullfrogs, I've been saving this empty frame for a photograph of a very special team. Any ideas who?"

"Melbourne Victory?" asked Jules.

"Manchester United?" asked Llama.

"My uncle's synchronised swimming group?" asked Stinkin' Lincoln.

Todd Turner sniggered.

"What? They're *very* good!' said Stinkin' Lincoln.

"No, none of that lot. See, this frame will hang pride of place here in our clubrooms, alongside all the valuable soccer memorabilia that I've collected over the years." said Coach Wentworth. "And the team that will feature inside it is…"

"Us." I said, stepping forward. Suddenly I got an attack of the chills.

"Correct, Rufus."

"I don't get it." said Stinkin' Lincoln.

"I'm going to put a photo of the *Bayview Bullfrogs* in this frame. Because today you're going to make *history*."

Principal Humpton smiled and locked his fingers over his stomach. "Wonderful," he said, munching on another orange.

"I pored over the history books last night and discovered that no Bullfrogs team has ever won the first game of any season." said Coach Wentworth.

"Really?" said Principal Humpton.

Coach Wentworth winked at him. He must've had something in his eye. "But that all changes today. So, tell me Bullfrogs, do you want to make *history*?"

"Yeah!" I cried, rubbing my hands together. "We know what we have to do."

But I was the only one talking. What was wrong with my teammates? I was the klutz who had stuffed up. I should've been the one moping about, not the others.

Happy Hughes shot me a look, as if to say, "We've heard it all before."

Coach Wentworth crouched down and glared at us through those big, magnified eyes, "This is a new season. Today we have the opportunity to write a new chapter in our history. I should know, after all I'm the acting vice-president of the State Soccer Historians Society. So, I'll ask you one more time, do you want to make *history*?"

Coach Wentworth's words hit home with me. I'd had enough of going half-hearted. This entire last month I'd been afraid of getting too involved in anything. Just in case the worst happened, which it mainly did, I have to admit. I was sick of it. I refused to be a catastrophe magnet any more.

I stood up, "Come on Bullfrogs, let's do this!"

"Yeah!" cried Dash.

"Totally dude!" said Jules.

And then I ridduped.

It was the sickest sounding frog noise you've ever heard but that didn't stop me. I just kept at it. "Riddup, riddup.". I was now a part of the team. And I wasn't keen on playing for a team that accepted losing.

Then Dash joined me ridupping. Then slowly, everyone else was at it. We all got to our feet and made the riddup noise. It echoed through the change room. And it sounded simply awful.

"That's more like it. Go out there and earn your place on the wall, Bullfrogs!" cried Coach Wentworth. "Make HISTORY!"

We burst onto the pitch in full voice.

15

GOAL HUNGRY

The Falcons were already in position as we took to the field. They must've been freaked out when they heard our riddups!

Principal Humpton obviously loved our coach's speech. As he left the clubrooms, he proudly patted Coach Wentworth on the back. Then Coach Wentworth patted Humpty on the back. Hard this time—Humpty was choking on an orange pip.

Llama waved her arms around to direct us in our new roles. There was a lot of talk about "zones" that I didn't understand. But I smiled a lot and even threw in a few thumbs ups.

Wheeeet! The ref blew her whistle and the second half was underway.

We came out firing. Pete intercepted the Falcon's kick off and passed out wide to Dash who immediately started sprinting down the wing. I'd never seen her so determined. Her eyes were WILD. It reminded me of the day Ruby pulled the tail of our new neighbour's cat.

Dash darted inside, using her speed to zoom past a Falcon defender. She chipped the ball to the top of the box. There were six players fighting for the ball. A flurry of boots, grass and mud. Then BANG! A goal!

"Woo hoo!" cried Principal Humpton from the sidelines.

"Marvellous!" cried Coach Wentworth. "Simply, marvellous!"

Mum was jumping up and down. "Go Bullfrogs," she cheered.

We all ran in in for high fives. (And chest bumps which caught me a little off guard.) Llama gave every one of us a hug. We jumped around and *riddupped* and soaked in all the cheers from our supporters. We'd actually done it! Even Happy Hughes cracked a grin.

No one was really sure who scored the goal, but both Frankie *and* Jules claimed it.

"Told you I was a gun!" yelled Jules, pretending to fire pistols in the air.

The score was now one-all. We'd levelled in less than a minute.

But more importantly, there was something different about my teammates. Scoring a quick goal had an immediate effect. There was a glint in their eye and a spring in their step. Suddenly they really *believed*. HISTORY was there for the taking.

Minutes ticked away. The Falcons weren't giving up without a fight. The second half was flying by. Both teams chipped the ball around, unable to get further shots on goal. It seemed to be just as difficult for the

Falcons as it was for us. The zone was working, but we were running out of time to get that winning goal.

Dash got me involved in the passes.

"Nice touch, Rufus!" Mum yelled from the crowd. "This is your chance, Bullfrogs!"

At first I was embarrassed but then I realised Mum was right. I'd slotted the ball through a tiny gap in the Falcons' defence. It hadn't been intentional but luckily Dash had speed on her side, and she sprinted through the opening, took my pass onside, and was zooming towards goal.

There was that mad look in her eye again. She was a bit like the Hulk, except she transformed into a GOAL HUNGRY MONSTER rather than a green one.

"Go Dash! Go!" I yelled.

"You can do it!" yelled Llama.

The Falcons goalie ran at Dash. She booted the ball. THUD!

It went straight through the goalie's hands, and smacked him right in the nose.

"Darn it!" I yelled.

The ball bounced clear to Dreadlocks.

"Come on! Now or never, Bullfrogs!" cried Coach Wentworth. "We're in extra time!"

Dreadlocks hoofed it long, but Todd Turner was able to win possession. He flicked the ball out wide so I could run on to it. I started dribbling with the whole field ahead of me.

This was the first time in the game I hadn't immediately passed off the ball. The air whooshed by as I strode forward. I felt the BUZZ again, the same feeling I had at the Socceroos match and at Archie Thompson's clinic. I ran and ran and ran, closing in on the goal.

But suddenly I became aware of everything around me. Dreadlocks and his mates closing in. Jules shouting to pass the ball to him. Spectators jumping up and down on the sidelines. Principal Humpty eating a hot dog. Birds flying overhead. The sun reflecting off the lake. And did I hear an animal grunting from a distance? Could it have possibly been a *bull*?

From the corner of my eye, I could see Mum cheering. And I froze. Again.

All the ways I could stuff this up were running through my head. All the ways this could end in DISASTER.

It was the same paralysing feeling from the night before when I'd been taking a penalty shot during the Socceroos match. I stood dead still. This was our last chance to win the game and I was sure I would totally muck it up.

But then I noticed Dash. And something inside me just clicked.

16

NO SUCH THING AS A NATURAL

There was no hearty slap on the back from an annoying announcer or any loud squawk from a passing crow this time. I had to do this all by myself. I could see Dash running towards the goal.

Calling on EVERY OUNCE of strength I had, I forced my leg to swing. I scooped up the ball, just as my Falcon opponent reached me. Half a second later he would've blocked my kick.

I fell to the ground. Everything seemed like it was slow motion.

The ball sailed through the air.

Dash was speeding forwards for my cross. I'd passed it

to her, just like I should've done in the car park the night before. The Falcon goalie was out of position as the ball landed at Dash's feet. Without wasting a micro-second she slammed it into the back corner of the net.

GOAAAAL!!!! 2-1. In extra time!

Luckily I was already on the ground for the celebrations. The Bullfrogs came from every position on the field for a stacks-on. I ended up a little too close to Stinkin' Lincoln's backside for my liking, but fortunately I was distracted by the INCREDIBLE winning feeling.

The ref blew the full time whistle.

WE HAD WON. And yes, I even scored a goal in my first match! Just not the type you brag about.

We shook hands with the Falcons and then all the Bullfrogs gathered in front of the clubrooms. Most of us dropped to the ground exhausted. I was a sweaty mess. I was sure I'd never stunk so much in all my life. And that included the day I fell into the pigpen. But it didn't matter for a single second.

"Best game ever." said Dash.

"Best *goal* ever." I said.

"Thanks." said Jules, thinking we were talking about the equalising goal that he had claimed. "Real soccer stars like me know how to turn it on when we need to."

Dash and I laughed.

"What's funny?" Jules asked.

"A stellar performance Bullfrogs! Well done indeed." said Coach Wentworth. "Gather round now, I want to take a photograph to remember this moment forever!"

Coach Wentworth took a photo of us, all whooping and hollering! This was the photo he had promised to take to fill that empty frame. We all posed. Even Tim Turner, with his injured leg propped before him.
I REALLY hoped my hair was in place.

Izzy gave me a nod, despite my "own goal". Which I took to mean: even though you scored a goal for the other team, in the end you helped our team eventually win, so you're okay by me. Izzy can say a lot with just a single nod.

Straight after the photo had been taken, Mum ran over and gave me a huge hug. And, weirdly, I wasn't even embarrassed. Dad, Rikki and Ruby had been watching the last few minutes from the supermarket, via Mum's smart phone. Was there no end to Mum's talent?

Dad had even worked out how to text back a set of thumbs up emojis.

"Proud of your son, Mrs Rogers?" asked Jules.
"I taught him that move."

"Did you now?" said Mum, smiling broadly.

"Yeah, I'm a natural." said Jules, then clicked his fingers and pointed to himself. "Cooler than *Kewell* some people say."

"There's no such thing as a natural. If you ask

me," said Mum. "I tend to think that to get good at
something, it's all about hard work, practice and belief."

Jules whispered to me, "Bor-*ring*."

But that's kind of what Dad had said too. I was
beginning to think they were right. Parents can be a bit
annoying like that.

Principal Humpton shook my hand. "Well done,
young Rufus. I'm so pleased to see you're settling in here
at Bayview."

"Thanks.' I said, then I turned to Mum. The rollercoaster match had left my emotions running high. I had
to get something off my chest. "I am so, so sorry I made
us move here from Biggins Valley, Mum."

"You?" she said, looking at me strangely.

"Yeah." I said. "After the incident with the bull."

"Oh, Rufus," said Mum crouching to my level. "You
didn't think we moved here to Bayview just because of
that, did you?"

"We didn't?"

"Of course not." said Mum, grabbing both my hands.
"We moved because I wanted to return to work now that
the girls are a little older. Plus the farm was becoming
a struggle. Our move had absolutely *nothing* to do with
that little mishap at your old school."

What? I'd been torturing myself about this ever since we'd got here. I dreamt about it almost every night. "Seriously?"

"Seriously." she said and hugged me again. "I'm so sorry you didn't realise."

THIS CHANGED EVERYTHING. Part of me didn't dare to believe it. I pulled out of the hug to search Mum's face.

"Honestly Rufus, we put the farm on the market over a year ago." said Mum. "A long time before that little incident."

Then—slowly—I smiled. And I think I may have relaxed my shoulders for the first time since we'd moved to Bayview. Suddenly, I felt like I could float away. But instead I hugged Mum again, tighter than I ever had before.

"Hey Soccerufus." said Dash. "Coach Wentworth wants you."

Coach Wentworth was holding something behind his back as he came towards us. Dash and Jules were grinning nearby.

"Master Rufus, you won this fair and square. And given how you got the Bullfrogs working together almost as well as the Aussies last night—don't think I didn't notice—I certainly can't think of anyone who deserves it more." said Coach Wentworth and he handed the signed Socceroos jumper back to me. He'd put it in a frame.

"Aw, wow! Thanks, Coach." I said, but as I grabbed it from him I accidently dropped it. Everyone gasped.

Dash caught it before it hit the ground.

PHEW!

Ding! sounded Coach Wentworth's jacket pocket. He took out his phone.

"Oh," he said. "I'm bidding online for a sweatband that belonged to the Brazilian soccer legend Pele, himself. Excuse me." He started reading out the text he was typing in reply. "Does it come with an autograph?"

"It was a great cross, Rufus. Well done." said Dash as she handed me back the Socceroos jumper. "We'll have to work on a few more smooth moves at training after school on Monday. Don't be l-l-late. Izzy likes to do penalty practice first thing. And she takes it pretty seriously."

I glanced over at Izzy. She locked eyes with me and tapped her wristwatch.

"I'll be there." I said and I gave Dash and Jules a high five.

That night I was TOTALLY pooped. It had been

a full-on couple of days. And I needed my sleep because I had a massive season of soccer ahead of me. I could sense the Bullfrogs were on the brink of a winning streak!

But I wouldn't stop there. In years to come, I was determined to be the one signing Aussie jumpers instead of winning them. All it would take was a bit of practice a lot of hard work, and stacks of belief and soon enough it would be me playing in the mighty green and gold.

Socceroos here I come.

Because the name's Rufus, SOCCERufus!

ARCHIE THOMPSON'S SOCCER SKILLS

TRAINING

The trick to becoming the best footballer that you can be, starts with training.

Here are my simple ideas for you to get the most out of your practice sessions.

1) Be on time and be prepared. A good attitude goes a long way!

2) If you cheat during the drills, even just a little, you're only cheating yourself.

3) Always warm up to avoid injury.

4) Practise your techniques correctly. Don't reinforce bad habits... If you're not sure, ASK!

LISTEN TO THE COACH

We have plenty of great coaches volunteering their time to lead young teams right across the country. Many of them have impressive football experience to share. So listen up and you might learn a thing or two!

1) Focus: the coach's advice can only be helpful if you're paying attention. Shut out all distractions and soak up their knowledge.

2) Follow the coach's directions even if you don't agree. It's okay to make suggestions but the coach has the final say. They have a clearer view of the bigger picture.

3) Ask questions! If you need some further explanation on something, the chances are that some of your teammates do as well. Good coaches are happy to help.

TEAM WORK

There's no "I" in team. (But there is an "AT"! Ha!) But seriously, one of the things I love most about football is that it truly is a team sport. Here are some pointers about teamwork.

1) A good team makes use of everyone's unique talents, rather than just relying on one or two players. Is your team fully utilising its different members?

2) Have you heard the phrase the 'sum is greater than the parts'? That's just a fancy way of saying that if you all work together, you can often achieve more than each of your individual efforts combined.

3) Football—like all sport—can be an emotional rollercoaster. But when you work as a team, lows are easier to take because you can share any difficulties with your teammates. And also, highs are better too, because you experience great times with your mates.

SET PLAYS

It's a huge thrill when a set play results in a goal. It means that all your hard work and tactics have paid off!

1) Know your role. Even if it is a minor part, each contribution is important.

2) Play your role. Don't get tempted to go for glory and ignore the team strategy. Trust in the plan.

3) If a set play fails, make sure you and the team try to work out why. Then you can tweak it to make it even better the next time.

PATIENCE

A bit of good old-fashioned patience can prove invaluable. Timing is everything, and if you get caught up in the moment it can often bring you undone. Here's my advice…

1) Sometimes skills training during a practice session can seem a little dull. But remember, if you're practising correctly and often enough, the skills you're working on will become second nature and will be a huge help to you during a game.

2) When attacking during a game, occasionally you have to bide your time until a good opportunity comes along. Unless the clock is against you, don't be afraid to chip the ball around and keep possession until the right moment comes to attack.

3) When defending during a game, there can be quiet times, especially if your team is doing all the attacking. Keep your mind on the game, run on the spot and stay in position. You and your co-defenders will need you

to be switched on and ready to defend should the opposition get a sudden chance to attack.

4) Sometimes seasons can seem way too long. Particularly if week after week, your team isn't having much luck out on the pitch. Hang in there. Football is a funny game. You only need a few things to go your way, and all of a sudden your next win is just around the corner.

SHOOTING FOR GOAL

If you're a striker, shooting for goal is the most important skill you can learn. But it can be trickier than it looks. Here are a few pointers:

1) Practise goal kicking for at least 15 minutes after every training session.

2) During a game, even if you're approaching the goal at top speed, always take the time to size up where you're going to kick the ball.

3) When you take your shot place the ball in, don't bang it in.

4) And when you kick a goal, always CELEBRATE!

GETTING PAST AN OPPONENT

Sometimes your best option is to take on your opponent, even though they're just as keen to steal the ball from you as you are to protect your possession. So, keep these tips in mind:

1) Resist the urge to slow down as you approach your opponent. That just makes it easier for them to tackle you.

2) Often a shimmy of the hips will fool a defender, allowing you to speed past them.

3) Or maybe take your best moves from the dance floor and use them on the pitch—that can work too!

4) But my personal secret: always wear a flashy pair of boots because they'll make you feel great and they'll get your opponent thinking you're a superstar!

HEADING THE BALL

Those new to soccer sometimes worry that heading the ball can hurt. Not true! (Mostly!) Rather than thinking, 'this is going to hurt', try thinking, 'I'm going to attack that ball'.

1) Keep yours eyes open! Seems obvious but it's a common mistake to go in blind.

2) Jump early. You need to get higher than everyone else.

3) Try to connect using your forehead—the sweet spot is just near the hairline.

4) Push your head through the ball upon contact, and don't be afraid to direct the ball downwards when going for goal. It'll be harder for the goalie to stop.

There you go, you'll be a soccer superstar in no time. But as I always say, my best advice for all you soccer nuts out there is just to have fun!

SOCCER 'DAD JOKES'

DOES YOUR DAD THINK HE'S THE FUNNIEST GUY IN THE WORLD? MINE TOO! WELL, HERE ARE SOME JOKES THAT ALL DADS ARE SURE TO LOVE.

BUT ARE THEY A CRACK UP? OR DO THEY BELONG IN A CHRISTMAS CRACKER?

YOU DECIDE.

WHY DID THE COW SCORE AN 'OWN GOAL'?
Because she thought her team was kicking in the udder direction!

WHY WAS THE WORST PLAYER IN THE SOCCER TEAM NICKNAMED CINDERELLA?
Because he ran away from the ball.

SOCCER 'DAD JOKES'

WHAT IS THE UNDERWEAR DRAWER'S FAVOURITE SPORT?
Sock-er!

**WHY WAS THE MAN WHO COULD ONLY WALK
IN STRAIGHT LINES SO BAD AT SOCCER?**
He always missed the corner.

**WHAT DID THE GIRLFRIEND SAY WHEN SHE FOUND
OUT HER BOYFRIEND WAS A GOALIE?**
He's a keeper!

**WHAT TASTES WORSE THAN PUTTING
AN OLD MOUTHGUARD IN YOUR MOUTH?**
Putting someone else's old mouthguard in your mouth.

WHY WAS EINSTEIN SO GOOD AT SCORING FROM CROSSES?
Because he always used his head.

WHY ARE BABIES NATURALS AT SOCCER?
Because they're such good dribblers.

WHY IS SOCCER THE SAFEST SPORT IN THE WORLD?
Because it's arm-less!

WHY ARE STRIPS OF WOOD GOOD FOR STOPPING GOALS?
Because they're always found in d'fence.

**WHAT'S THE NAME OF THE SOCCER COMPETITION
FOR HORSES?**
The Neigh League!